Nightmare's Fairy Tale

SHOAH STUDIES

Alan L. Berger
Series Editor

Nightmare's Fairy Tale

A Young Refugee's Home Fronts, 1938–1948

Gerd Korman

THE UNIVERSITY OF WISCONSIN PRESS

The University of Wisconsin Press
1930 Monroe Street, 3rd Floor
Madison, Wisconsin 53711-2059

www.wisc.edu/wisconsinpress/

3 Henrietta Street
London WC2E 8LU, England

5   4   3   2

Printed in the United States of America

Library of Congress Cataloging-in-Publication Data
Korman, Gerd.
    Nightmare's fairy tale : a young refugee's home fronts, 1938–1948 /
    Gerd Korman.
    p.   cm.—(Shoah studies)
  Includes bibliographical references and index.
  ISBN 0-299-21080-4 (cloth: alk. paper)
    1. Korman, Gerd—Childhood and youth.   2. Jewish
children—Poland—Biography.   3. Holocaust, Jewish
(1939–1945)—Poland—Zbaszyn—Personal narratives.
4. Korman family.   5. Kindertransports (Rescue operations)—
England.   6. Refugees, Jewish—England—Exeter—Biography.
7. Holocaust survivors—New York (State)—New York—Biography.
8. Zbaszyn (Poland)—Biography. 9. East New York (New York,
N.Y.)—Biography.   I. Title.   II. Series.
DS135.P63K5695   2005
940.53'18'092—dc22   2005011891

ISBN 0-299-21084-7 (pbk.: alk. paper)

The author is grateful to the following institutions for permission
to reproduce their photographs: American Jewish Committee, the
newspaper Aufbau, Cornell University Library Archive, New York
City Municipal Archive, University of St. Louis Archive, Yad Vashem,
and YIVO. David McHugh of Hampton Photos made prints of
personal photographs.

To
THE GRANDCHILDREN
of
MAX and ROSA LAUFER KORMAN:
may their children flourish ❧

Contents

Illustrations

Nightmare's Fairy Tale

Prologue

The picture postcard from the ocean liner *Washington* had an odd address, but obviously it was meant to go to England. So on April 30, 1940, a postal clerk in Brooklyn sent it on its way, back across the dangerous wartime waters of the Atlantic. An English postal clerk recognized "Talaton," added Exeter, Devon, and sent it forward. In Talaton the mailman corrected the mistakes my mother had made in Genoa, Italy, just before boarding the *Washington* for New York City. She had addressed the card to her sons, "Herrn Gerd u. Manfred," left a space, added "Korman," left another space, and wrote "Talaton," using a bolder script and underlining it, before adding "England" below the line with the hook at the end. It was then she must have realized she needed the family name of the person with whom she thought we were staying. Between "Gerd u Manfred" and "Korman" she squeezed in "b/Cottage." In the message section at the top—above the identification of the *Washington*'s service between New York and European ports as being "temporarily transferred" by the latest neutrality act "to the New York–Genoa–Naples route"—she added the greeting "Gruss an Miss Cottage." My mother's trust in Talaton, England, was not misplaced, even though Britain was now at war with Germany and her postcard was written in German. No clerk had trashed it! And in tiny Talaton they had fixed the mistakes. Someone had decoded the address: Gerd u. Manfred, two of the little Kindertransport boys from Poland, who had come with the Jewish evacuees from London; Cottage was Rose Cottage, and Miss Cottage was either Polly Gosling or her daughter Ruth, who lived in Rose Cottage on Whimple Road, just off the junction leading into the village. They had taken in the boys and were helping them to recover from a nightmare executed in broad daylight.

Amid strands of emotionally charged memory and a historian's quest for private and public papers, Mutti's postcard is still in transit. It is an icon in the pasts of my present tenses. It comes from an emotional natal event lasting about a decade: a homeland without invested scapes of land or town, a homeland without a sense of place; a was and is of my own construction, which, without a sense of exile, is still full of mythic cords entangling family and strangers, some of whom came close.

The postcard also travels in the company of other icons that represent the pain of others, for which our age has achieved so much tolerance; and, oh yes, in the company of icons representing a world beyond pain, a world of cinders to which some of us pay homage, hoping desperately to make a difference.

Over the years those associations changed the impact of my mother's postcard even as it travels in its singularity. By the end of World War II, I had read and heard about other nightmares that made ours something quite different from what I thought it was. And, later, when reports of deportations and refugees continued to pour in from all over, this particular story about a refugee family, its commitments in solitary struggles, was no longer young.

Yet the telling of it retains a remarkable and instructive migration story, at least so it seems to me, an American historian reflecting on his influence-laden childhood. Between 1933 and 1948 important individuals and events touched me directly— such as rites of passage and the recurring Passover festival— some of which I have used to structure this narrative. Others are secular. For example, in 1933 my uncle Oswald Laufer, Mutti's brother, was executed gangland-style by paramilitary Nazis. Today a plaque authorized by the Social Democratic Party to which he belonged commemorates the site of his assassination.

A different kind of event occurred in 1938. That year Germany deported my family to the eastern frontier, together with some eighteen thousand other Polish Jews. Nowadays historians consider this act as one of the key events foreshadowing the Nazi regime's forced-deportation practices during the war.

Another incident occurred in 1939, when my father sailed on the German steamship *St. Louis* from Hamburg to Cuba, which had to turn around and sail back to Germany. He was forced to end this well-publicized journey in Holland's Westerbork, which the German occupiers later turned into a notorious transit camp. It sent thousands to their deaths, including Anne Frank and Etty Hillesum.

The last example comes from an extraordinary encounter for a son devoted to his parents. In the 1970s and 1980s I learned about my father's intimate wartime friendship with Etty in Westerbork through letters, a diary, and conversations. In the 1980s, when her diary and letters were published posthumously, Etty achieved an international reputation as a kind of postmodern saint.

My version of this American immigration story is instructive. It has a lot to say about the place of commitments in a young person's struggle to retain familiar yet changing collective identities of a people and of a family, not only in the traumatic days of deportation and wartime separation in Europe but also during the longer years of adjustment to American life in New York City.

This story also helped me to better account for my professional involvement in the study of the Holocaust. For that reason I conclude with an epilogue that tries to unravel a complex tangle of motivation prompted, on the one hand, by my nightmare years and, on the other, by my sense of professional obligation. Together they stirred me to teach and write about the Holocaust as early—which is late—as the mid-1960s.

I begin within an American immigrant tradition, with an account of a return visit to private European battlegrounds many years later.

Part I

The Battlegrounds

1

Fifty-three years after our deportation, Manfred and I went back. The specific reason was that the year before a family wedding deeply connected to the war years had stimulated travel conversations between us: Prague? Berlin? Maybe even Hamburg and . . . ?

By then we had multiplied and had buried our closest. Pappi died in 1962, felled by a heart attack at age sixty-four, too young to be pressed by his five grandchildren with difficult questions about his past. Manny phoned with the news at 2 A.M. By 10 A.M. we were exiting the Delancey Street subway station on the Lower East Side of Manhattan, where Shimen Korman, a second cousin, was waiting at the head of the stairs. Manny had called him and he, in turn, had insisted we meet him before going to the funeral parlor. After a long embrace, he gave us instructions that were brief but to the point: "Don't let him sell you expensive boxes. Tell him you want a simple pine box. Simple. Nothing fancy. A simple pine box. That's what Social Security covers and that is all you need." Then he went on his way to make all sorts of other arrangements; for it was Friday and Pappi had to be buried quickly, out in Queens, so that the Sabbath observers like Shimen could go to the cemetery and come back before sundown. Some old friends had come with their World War II memories of days shared in Holland's Westerbork, but there had not been time for anything but a small family gathering. A few cars traveled to Queens, and there, after the last ritual, we buried Pappi amid his kinfolk.

Mutti died twenty-one years later, struck down by a stroke. Without ever having forgotten Jerusalem, her right hand lost its cunning and her tongue cleaved to the roof of her mouth. For three long years courageous Mutti managed to talk with her eyes and hand and by forcing sounds out of her mouth. She had been so excited when her brother Sally had come from England to visit her. Then she suddenly quit eating and died, still attached to a breathing machine. We buried her next to Pappi, far removed from the Europeans who had brought them so much pain and suffering, among his relatives from the Galician town of Narol. They had helped her in the "Fun City" she came to love, the city where her six grandchildren had visited her often and where, in the last year, she met her first great-grandchild.

A year before that wedding I had also become a widower. In Ruthie's last days she had met the future bride, but not long enough to learn about the remarkable connection between her and our family. I heard about it on a November Sabbath in Los Altos Hills, California, which a few days earlier had been struck by an earthquake of its own.

During that lovely Shabbat afternoon at the home of Siobhan Fink, who was engaged to Joshua, we were schmoozing in a spacious living room while sitting on a big sofa in front of a coffee table piled high with photo albums. Many of the pictures had been taken in the Bay Area, where Siobhan had grown up; a few were of her father, Aaron, in his hometown of Chicago, and a lot had been taken in Toronto, where her mother, Zelda, lived. "And this is my uncle—Cass," Siobhan said, turning the page to move along to others. I had missed the first name and Cass in the Fink household did not register. But her mother wanted me to know some details about this man, whom she called Sam. "He was one of my brothers from Toronto, where I come from." There had been a terrible car accident, killing him and his family. "He served as chaplain in the Canadian army. His unit fought in parts of Holland." I went blank. Siobhan turned the picture over so that I could read the name: "Cass." I heard my faltering voice saying: "Do you know who this is? Do you know? It's the chaplain who wrote to Miller Avenue in Brooklyn from Westerbork. Joshie! You are marrying Rabbi Cass's niece!"

This wedding was the third in our Ithaca, New York, family; like the weddings of Manfred and myself and the bar and bat mitzvahs of our children, it occasioned great joy and celebration. Mutti had lived long enough to see a video of her first granddaughter's wedding. A few years later Ruthie had danced at her last family celebration. Now, without her, we were part of a

Family wedding picture taken at the marriage of Malkie and Gavin in 1994. In addition to my children and grandchildren, plus the children of Manfred and Mona Korman, this photograph includes: Ann Sandford, my best friend of many years, and her son Paul Guggenheim; Korman cousins from Narol; Murray and Claire Zloten, Ruth's brother and his wife; Ruth Kornfeld, a friend from Elmira, N.Y.; and Tobi Gussow, an Engelberg cousin from Miller Avenue in Brooklyn.

traditional kosher wedding in a California winery, sharing in an extraordinary event. That a grandson of Max Korman should find and marry the niece of Chaplain Cass—who in 1945 had written Mutti on Miller Avenue that Pappi was alive—seemed impossible!

That's why weddings are made in heaven," was the comment of the mystically inclined. The next generations were all in attendance. Arona and Gadi came from Rehovot with Amit, Avner, and Avital; and later Arona gave birth to Ruthie and David. Ezra and Andy came from Jerusalem with Liav; and later Andy gave birth to Aviad and Shani. Malka, who married Gavin, came from Rochester, New York; and later Malka gave birth to Moshe and

Raphael. Manfred came, and also Mona and their two sons, Clifford and Jerry. Clifford married Natalia and Jerry married Mira; and later Mira gave birth to Ariel and Benjamin and Natalia to Darius. Siobhan gave birth—yes, later she gave birth—to Raquel, Jaime, Shaine, and Tova.

Manfred and I had planned our European trip as relatively relaxed American tourists. He wanted to visit Berlin and I was eager to go to recently freed Prague. In fact, visits to these two cities were our excuses to return not to a homeland of emigration (like so many other immigrants) but to streets, buildings, and playing fields that we associated with our European experiences between 1938 and 1940. We also wanted to visit a cemetery in Wuppertal, in the Rhineland, where Mutti's murdered brother Oswald was laid to rest.

Years earlier—I in 1969, Manfred in 1971—we had been in Hamburg, each with our own families. I had run away; he had enjoyed himself. We had always had different experiential memories of our deportation and migration, and in the intervening years we had been affected by our own families' collective outlook. This time would be quite different; now, as then, we would be leaning on each other. We were going alone, two brothers without their families, walking where we had played as children, he hardly seven and I barely ten years of age. I had even found a treasured old black and white photograph of an event neither of us recalled, which showed us playing with our neighbor Christian Geisler's children all dressed up in fashionable sailor outfits. In 1939 their father had saved Pappi's life by helping him gain passage on the ill-fated *St. Louis,* and in 1940 he saved Mutti's life by arranging her voyage on the *Washington.*

As soon as we had boarded a British Airways flight in New York, I became anxious. In front of us sat a mother and a four-year-old son talking in German about visiting Oma and Opa. I reminded Manfred of my earlier failed efforts with Germany—not with individual Germans but with Germany, the land and Germans considered as a collective body.

One summer, on the way back to the United States from a 1968–69 sabbatical leave in Israel, my family and I arranged to leave from Copenhagen because our Volvo's leaking roof required repair in a Volvo garage. In making the reservations, I did not realize what that decision would mean emotionally: after sailing from Israel to Venice, we would have to drive through Italy, Switzerland, and then through Germany. North of Basel it finally hit me: I was about to drive on the Autobahn, the German superhighway, which would connect us to Lübeck, where we would take the ferry to Denmark.

Although we were all passengers in transit, I felt uneasy. I was in trouble from the moment we reached the kiosk. When the car ahead of us rolled back a bit, barely touching my bumper, I got out to inspect the damage. "Its nothing, its nothing," one of the officials reassured me in German. I responded in English—only English—expressing my absurd concern as I gazed at the guard and the driver accusingly. The event signaled the beginning of a recurrent pattern for as long as I remained on German soil. I scrutinized everyone who appeared older than forty and fused that person with their "evil" past. Then, when we reached Hamburg, my children wanted to see where I had lived and gone to school. For a moment I hesitated, looking desperately toward Ruth, even as I drove into the city.

Within minutes I was in familiar surroundings but had overshot the street where I used to live. I stopped, and out of nowhere another car appeared. In accented English its young, blond, blue-eyed driver asked if he could help. Inexplicably I replied in German, without any of the malaise I had experienced since leaving Basel. For a moment I felt like an ordinary tourist—but just for a moment.

It was dusk when a crisis loomed. I saw the street name Bornstrasse. A few years later I wrote about this visit.

I glanced left for the street sign of the famous Bornplatz, whose name my synagogue had also carried. No Bornplatz!!! This was now the home of Hamburg's university. Surely someone would remember. I asked a woman passing by, stared at her, and understood everything when she responded with a curt yes to my question, "Is that where the Bornplatz used to be?" I drove across the street and, stopping in a little square, saw a strange, unfamiliar street name above me. There was no more Bornplatz. Then I lost control: "I will not get out of this car. We will not get out of this car. The wheels have to touch this soil, but we do not," I screamed, throwing the car in gear. As I fled from German soil, my family remained silent.[1]

I visited Germany again in 1980 to do some research at the Institute for Contemporary History in Munich. At the time I was on leave from Cornell University and was teaching about the Holocaust at the Oxford Centre for Hebrew and Jewish Studies. It seemed an opportune moment to "hop over" for some interviewing and study of Wehrmacht records on foreign labor in wartime Germany, a project I had started earlier in the year. However, it was only after I had boarded the British Airways plane, with lots of German-speaking businessmen aboard, that I fully understood my self-deception: "hop over" indeed. I could not stop the cascade of memories from the Bornplatz. While working at the Institute, I managed to focus on the manuscripts, but once outside the archive this proved impossible. Within thirty-six hours after my arrival, I checked out of the hotel and fled, accompanied by the song "Hallelujah," Israel's victorious entry in that year's Eurocontest, which was blaring out of the loudspeaker—in Hebrew!—in the bus taking me to the airport.

I also told Manfred about the 1968 Westerbork experience, which he had never visited. It started at the Anne Frank House in Amsterdam, where no one seemed to know Westerbork's location. Persistent questioning brought irritation from the young men and women assigned to deal with pesky tourists. They were much more interested in using Holocaust language for mobilizing opinion on behalf of their anticolonial crusades than they were concerned about Anne and Westerbork. They did not know where the camp was and could not have cared less.

Locating the village of Westerbork on our maps, we headed in the direction of northeastern Holland. In Assen, the largest town in the vicinity of the village, we again asked for directions a number of times, but no one seemed to know about the camp, only the village; mention of the camp brought blank stares. At first we thought our ignorance of Dutch was at fault, but then it became obvious that many with whom we spoke understood our English or German. Even in the village of Westerbork we could not get directions. Finally, in a restaurant just off one of the main roads, the owner sort of stared at me and asked: "The old Jodenkamp, you mean the old Jodenkamp?"

The camp in Westerbork was still intact, smaller than in 1942 but now being used to shelter Moluccans, interned refugees from the former Dutch holdings in Indonesia, who were living in the same kinds of barracks Pappi had known. We drove in and out before finding the water tower and railhead marking the beginning of the spur line inside Westerbork, the starting point of the transports. Alone we would not have found it, but we saw a car with a Dutch registration plate cruising slowly ahead of us. When it stopped, we questioned the driver and he knew exactly where everything was; he and his compatriots came regularly to these grounds on pilgrimage. They told us about plans for reforestation of the whole area and agreed that there were no markers or signs indicating what had happened here. Perhaps after the Moluccans leave, but who knows.

Just then Ezra, almost seven, came running up in tears. By mistake he had closed all of the car doors—with the keys still inside! Our Dutch fellow visitors walked us back to the four-door Volvo and tried to figure out how to open one of the doors. I was much too nervous to hold a wire hanger steady enough to insert it inside the window and lift the doorknob. Trapped, I thought, in vastly different circumstances than Pappi had been, but still trapped, with the sun sinking ever closer to the horizon. Soon it will be dark. What then, I wondered, and missed the knob again. One of the Dutch visitors was calmer and more agile. He looped a string, squeezed it through the small opening of the window, caught the latch, and pulled the knob up. Soon we were on our way again, out of the old Jodenkamp.

As the pilot began his approach to Hamburg, Manfred reassured me. "I have been here before, no problem. You'll be fine. It's a gorgeous city. Make like a tourist." Halfheartedly I replied. "Right. Tourists. So from the time we land we should speak German," which we did often, especially in the streets, shops, and hotels. But in using German in Hamburg I felt differently than when I had used the language as a German speaker outside Germany. I could not ignore the hidden meaning in which each word seemed couched when it was uttered across a counter or under a lamppost. I just knew that this stranger behind the baggage counter, that clerk in a boutique, or the waiter at an outdoor cafe did not want to know when I left Germany or how old I was then because my answers would create a permanent barrier to further conversation—and might even block a sale.

Except for a general geographical orientation, which anyone

reading a map could have obtained, this lovely city gave me no feeling of belonging: I belonged to people, not to bricks and stones. *Heimat* was not here, where Manfred and I walked our feet off. We found "our" familiar street names (Rotebaumschussee, Grindelallee, Behnstrasse, Heidberg, Kronskampf) and landmarks (the Hamburg Sportverein's soccer stadium, the Stadtpark, railway stations, and the Alster Pavillon), only to wonder how we really related to these places. To me they were all fossils of the mind combined with memories of Mutti's stories, intertwined with what I saw in front of me, representations by urban planners and builders who reconstructed the city after World War II. (In 1971 Manfred had experienced the precision of that reconstruction. Mutti had given him travel instructions based on her recollections of prewar Hamburg. They were as reliable in 1971 as they had been for Mutti in 1938.) The HSV stadium, which I associated with a visit from Himmler—Manfred and I had attended one of the league games by crawling through a hole in the fence—was now a training field, the main stadium having been moved to the edge of the city. We realized that fact only after we had begun to reminisce in front of a fence through which we had crawled long ago. Sometimes urban developers had let "our" buildings stand: the small apartment house opposite our apartment, from whose windows Manfred and I had seen a construction worker fall from the fifth floor to the sidewalk below; the Heidberg complex was also still standing as it had in the early 1930s, when Manfred grew out of diapers and I started to commute to my day school.

As we crossed one particular street, we were excited to read a familiar name: Herbert Weichmann Strasse. "That's Frankie's uncle's street," we both exclaimed as we remembered the family friend who had become a famous Social Democrat—Uncle Oswald's party—in Hamburg and in greater Germany. He surely deserved to be honored, this remarkable educator and politician who, when being considered for president of West Germany, rejected the idea. In the late 1960s in Israel, where he represented Germany at the funeral of Premier Levi Eshkol, he told me it was too soon after World War II for a Jew to serve Germany in that capacity.

The Bornplatz and my school, the famous Talmud Torah Schule, connected me in a different way, but even here I remained uninvolved, observing, making bloodless connections. I walked on the two-dimensional architectural rendering of the synagogue carved into the stone of the plaza named after Joseph Carlebach, chief rabbi of Hamburg. As a child I had danced with him. Following his deportation, the Germans murdered him. There had been markers neither in 1969 nor two years later, when Manfred had come to visit. I thought to myself: This named plaza is better, but I don't know why. It's good to see the old name of the school engraved in bold letters on the stone of the old building, which now housed a library school. Inside, on the first floor, "they" retained the relief, listing the fallen faculty and students who had served in the German army before the Nazi revolution. I wondered why.

As a strolling tourist, I enjoyed the experience of having a coffee with Manfred overlooking the Alster, inner Hamburg's famous artificial lake. Mutti loved to do just that; the view was stunning. When I listened to the Italian-accented German waiter take our order, the German words seemed to become less irritating. I said something about it to Manfred. His response made my day: "This is 1991. Subtract 1945 and you get forty-six. Anyone forty years or older in 1945 is now at least eighty-six years old; thirty years in 1945 is seventy-six years old. Almost all the Nazi bad guys are dead or too old to matter."

Manfred's attitude toward his Hamburg past was different from mine: he had none of my hang-ups. He was a successful junior high school principal from Queens, New York, expressing genuine accomplishment at having reconnected with his first school and synagogue. Where I was ambivalent he was triumphant, remembering specific events conjured up by a corner of a courtyard or corridor. Where I saw no use in telling strangers who we were—I was convinced they would not want to go back to our time—Manfred took delight in announcing who he was. "Sure," he said to me, "I want them to know. I am back, an American Jew who made it, proud and strong. Take it or leave it. I don't care."

His triumphant American enthusiasm was a wonderful celebration of continental paths not traveled from Zbaszyn: into the interior of Poland's Galicia, no doubt to Narol, where—with Pappi's parents, brother, in-laws, nieces, and nephews—we would have faced the Nazi rule that brought death to all but a few of our extended family; or into an Otwock future, a makeshift Kindertransport center outside Warsaw, with those who had to stay behind—there, too, we would have had a short life. And elsewhere in central Europe—even in a Germany without a Nazi revolution—we who were not among the best and brightest would never have experienced the world of higher education, not with the means and connections available to our East European Jewish family. In that sense New York City was unparalleled: free high schools, free superb colleges, and the various other opportunities that all sorts of Americans made available to us white Jewish boys.

From Hamburg we drove toward Westerbork, appreciating that in Holland the camp had been integrated into Dutch public life. Unlike in 1968, a far-off highway directional sign now guided us to a museum and control center. All had changed, I thought, and wondered how this center fit into Europe's twisted Jewish museum culture. Silently I speculated about the following juxtaposition: the old camp site, along whose perimeter large satellite dishes were visible, mute expressions of a civilization desperate to comprehend the unknown. A bit like myself and Pappi and this place, especially Pappi and the by then famous Etty Hillesum and their Westerbork friendship.

Manfred did not say much; he was clearly overwhelmed by this, his first visit. It was a real place, not a figment of his imagination. In the museum, where pictures were everywhere, he searched for Pappi or any of his friends that Manfred had known, anybody to make the connection real. We talked to the director, but except for Etty he recognized none of their names. Manfred had it right when he glanced through the lists of deportees who had died in death camps: "Here they are not interested in the survivors, only the dead ones."

Zbaszyn was scary—it always is. Driving in a rented car, we approached it from Berlin, more or less along the same route that the railway had brought us in 1938. After crossing the border at Frankfort on the Oder, we drove some thirty miles or so along Highway E30 while looking for the junction for Zbaszyn. We felt alienated, in hostile country. I worried about American media stories of antisemitism and muggings of tourists in post-Soviet

Poland. "I know why we did not prepare for this part of the trip," I said to Manfred, who was taking his turn at the wheel. "I didn't want to read about Zbaszyn, not before, not now, and not tomorrow." Nevertheless, we persisted, even stopping to take a picture of a "Zbaszyn" sign before going into the town.

In the end we even found nearby little Nadnia, with its cobblestone-paved streets and mud ruts with which we had lived for a few months. We drove a few meters down a narrow lane to our old lakeshore, where neighbors had fished and where we had celebrated our Nadnia seder. With Zbaszyn at its northern tip, the whole scene suggested a bedroom suburb for Poznan, several miles farther east. Late in the afternoon, just before returning to Berlin, we stood for a moment in the empty hall of the small railway station, observing the trains coming in from Germany and heading east toward Warsaw.

We had been prisoners here for almost a year, but we didn't try to find the no-man's-land we had crossed, the stables, or the flour mill in which we had been quartered. We walked away without saying a word to anyone. Not once did we speak about going on to Otwock, which we remembered all too well:

Rotten tomatoes for lunch
   Refugee kids have the runs
To hell with their latrine
   Go bare-assed!
Against the window screen

Talaton in England's Devon was glorious. The ride on motorway M5 from Heathrow was wildly exhilarating, free of the oppressiveness I had not been able to shake while on the Continent. Now I was the returning tourist, thrilled to tell everybody who we were: Talaton boys from the early war days. Wherever we stopped in Devon, our English hosts always wanted to go back to "our time," to talk about 1939–40; young and old alike, they wanted to know the details, the more the better.

Near Talaton we checked into a roadside hotel and almost immediately went to say a quick hello to Freda Frajdenreich, one of our "sisters" from Poland. In the event, we stayed late into the night, learning much about her since the war: her sister Paula had moved north, away from the Talaton area, while she and her husband Pete Richards had found comfort and a sense of well-being for themselves and their children here. She talked to us about the abandonment she and her sister had felt. When they began to comprehend the meaning of silent parents and relatives during and after the war, she and her sister needed to convert to their new parents' religion. Freda did have limited contact with our Kindertransport brother Yossel Kamiel; and in the last few years she had become involved in reunions for youngsters like us, who had come to England on a Kindertransport. However, for most of the evening we talked about the triumph: recovery and the ability to build a new life.

On the following day Manfred and I went to Talaton. There we introduced ourselves: to a storekeeper who happened to be related to the Gosling family; to a well-to-do farmer who "of course" remembered the Jewish evacuees from London ("There were some from Poland, you know"); and to the artist who now lived in what once had been the little school at the bottom of the hill. We passed the town hall and found the lanes that were supposed to lead to Rose Cottage, where we had lived for a year.

I reminded Manfred of my last visit here, when I had been teaching in Oxford. "We all came in a rented van, traveling on the road from Ottery St. Mary. I found the junction with Whimple Road, turned left, and looked for the cottage on my right. It was gone, but I knew it had to be there. Frenzied, I turned that big van around in one of those narrow lanes. I drove back ever so slowly and concluded that the cottage had stood where all that construction was occurring on my left. I stopped the van, got out, and headed toward the entrance. At the same time a guy driving a tractor was coming out of the driveway. He stopped in front me as I called up to him: 'Is this where the old Rose Cottage stood?' He leaned down and asked in a surprised voice: 'Manfred?' It was Henry Peters, your old buddy! So who knows what we'll find today. Everything has been remodeled and rebuilt."

Just then we turned off the lane we had been following and onto a narrower track between two houses. A step or two from the small staircase leading up to a house on the right a big man, whom I did not recognize, was coming down. So we asked him if the property next to his included the land where Rose Cottage once stood. "Manfred," he replied. We had stumbled onto Henry and his house! All these years he had been living next door. He

showed us exactly where Rose Cottage had stood and then insisted we come into his home to meet his wife and sons.

There we learned something we had not known about the
Peters family and, by extension, about some of the people living in Talaton when we had been refugees and evacuees there.
Ruth Gosling, one of our Talaton mothers, who had named Yossel "Joe," had once written to us: "Mrs. Peters always asks for
you both when she sees Joe."[2] We thought it was just a kindly
neighbor's interest, and no doubt it was that too. But Henry said
he knew we would return one day and meet again because, well,
because in some way it was all part of God's plan. He seemed to
belong to an Exeter Christian sect predisposed to convert Jews.
Sooner or later he just knew we'd meet and who knew what
would happen then. As I recorded his remarks, he reminded
Manfred: "I remember something I believe. It always stayed in
my memory that my mother gave you a New Testament when
you left, a little pocket book. I am sure she used to do such things
as that. She was a God-fearing lady, and my parents, without a
shadow of a doubt. I had a feeling that's what she did because
she was always giving away literature, Christian literature."
Stunned and not wanting to act the spoiler, Manfred agreed, but
afterward he told me he had no idea what Henry was talking
about. "Who knows, maybe she did." Before we left his house
and said our good-byes Henry thanked "our Lord and Savior
Jesus Christ" for all the good deeds and kindnesses in our Talaton past and for this time that we were spending with his family.
It was a special moment, warm and friendly—even moving.

We had one other surprise waiting for us when we met Yossel
and his wife, Helen, for lunch at a kosher restaurant in down-
town London. While driving there, I remembered my first reunion with him in 1967 and his help in arranging a meeting with
Miss Gosling.

Following the Six-Day War, on the way back from an emotional trip to Israel, I had stopped in London to meet Uncle Sally,
find Yossel and, hopefully, Miss Gosling. While a soldier during
World War II, Sally had married. After returning to civilian life,
he had managed to open a small shop in London's garment district. I now met his wife, Sara, and their young son, Stephen. Together we reminisced about Talaton, his army service, and life

behind a sewing machine in the East End. They helped me locate Yossel. Following a telephone conversation, in no time at all he was downstairs waiting for me in his Rover.

On the way over to his house in Golders Green, he brought me up to date, describing the reunion with his mother and sister, his recent marriage, and the arrival of his first child, born a year ago. He also told me of his extraordinary business successes, making it possible for him to own a Rover, a home in expensive Golders Green, and to buy another one for his mother, who lived next door. By the time he introduced me to Helen and to little Jonathan, I was overwhelmed with joy.

"It wasn't until a couple of years ago that I began to make peace with being Jewish. That's when I met Helen and here we are," he said proudly while looking at his baby son in the crib. He also explained the Rover. One of the companies he worked for as a bookkeeper had struck it rich during London's booming early 1960s and took him to the top. By the time of our reunion, he had become an important figure in the firm.

Through regular visits and the installation of a telephone in Rose Cottage, Yossel had stayed in close touch with Ruth Gosling; he could therefore give me precise instructions regarding how and when to reach the cottage: "Go by train from Paddington to Exeter and there take a hired car. Tell the driver to wait because you don't want to spend more than about forty-five minutes. She'll be expecting you because I shall telephone ahead. She's too frail for surprises like you arriving at her door."

Except for the feeling that I had been here before, on the journey out from Paddington I felt like a tourist—that is, until the driver dropped me off. There were some geese nearby, but I was alone that morning, walking down the path from the road toward the small door of the tiny cottage. As had been my meeting with Yossel when I was about to greet him, I felt so ashamed that I had not stayed in touch with Ruth Gosling, especially after Mutti had made her pilgrimage. We owed her so much, I thought, as I knocked on the door. A tiny, slightly emaciated but smiling woman bid me enter. I kissed her cheek, and felt tears well up as I followed her past the narrow cot on which she slept, together with her big dog, who was stretched out on this bed, which they shared. "My God," I thought, "there is hardly any room for her."

By then we were in the kitchen, where she invited me to partake of the lunch she had prepared. Like the rest of the cottage, the kitchen was sparsely furnished, but everything she needed was there. Plates, napkins, and cutlery were on the wooden table, as were the cheese, bread, and fresh vegetables. "You see, Gerhard," she said as she poured the hot tea, "I didn't forget." The frail mistress of Rose Cottage had served no meat on this day, eighteen years after we had first met. During the meal I asked all sorts of questions, but there was no conversation, just as Yossel had predicted. He knew his Talaton mother well. She permitted me to see some of the other rooms, including "ours," with its window looking out on a tall walnut tree, following which we said good-bye. By evening I was back at Sally's, jumbling the events of the day: I just did not know how to share my emotional turmoil with them, for I knew I would never see Ruth Gosling again.

In the restaurant we reminisced and talked a lot about our Talaton days. But when I started to ask some questions about our Talaton seder with water, Yossel said he did not know what I was talking about. I looked at Manfred while Helen stared at us, and then I said to Yossel in sheer disbelief: "You don't remember the seder? Did you know we ate no meat for most of that first year?" No, he did not remember that three of us had been a Jewish presence in Rose Cottage.

Now I began to understand—perhaps for the first time—my role in Devon's Talaton. He and Manfred had been too young to establish any kind of presence representing family practices and traditions. Although I had been just a few years older, I was old enough. When we left for America in 1940, Yossel—and, for that matter, Paula and Freda—remained alone. Abandoned! It was a chilling thought, this awareness of the difference a little boy of eleven had made in the home of Miss Cottage of Talaton.

There was one loose end that still needed tying up after we came home. We had also visited the grave of Oswald, Mutti's heroic murdered brother. Before 1933, as a member of the Social Democrats and of the Reichsbanner, a militant wing of Social Democrats, he had fought local Nazis in the streets in order to defend his party's values and property. His gravesite was in a well known cemetery but I wondered how many of Wuppertal's few remaining Jews ever came here and got off at the bus stop called "Jewish Cemetery"? It was divided into four parts. There was the old cemetery, with its headstones dating from the 1930s and from earlier decades. At a lower level was a new section, dating from 1945. It included many who had returned after the war or had been buried in Elberfeld after having lived abroad. Among these headstones were others, collectively forming a third section that included contemporary residents reared in Elberfeld since the war. Finally, there was a fourth section that had no headstones at all, representing the hundreds who had lived here as late as 1940, when Mutti, en route to the United States, had to abandon Oma and Opa. These Jewish dead had no individual markers. Instead, a memorial stone at the entrance explained why the years on the headstones skipped from 1939 to 1945.

During our first visit we could not find the grave in the old section, where Oswald had been buried by his parents in 1933. Perhaps if Uncle Sally had been well, the search would have been easier, but his Parkinson's disease had become acute. (On his eightieth birthday we flew to London to celebrate the event; he died a few years later.) I was prepared to abandon this search. "Let's declare it found," I suggested, "the way we declared our Behnstrasse apartment found on another block in Hamburg where we had located a house that looked more or less like the one we thought we had lived in years ago." Manfred would have none of it. He had to find as many demonstrable and verifiable physical links as he could to connect him to his family's past. The following day we found our way to the office of Wuppertal's or-ganized Jewry, which provided sufficient information for us to locate the grave during a second visit to the cemetery. We had stood next to it, had photographed the headstone, but because of overgrown shrubbery we had not seen the family name Laufer.

This experience induced me to undertake a task Mutti had not been able to complete. In 1964 she had tried in vain to persuade Wuppertal's mayor to recognize publicly the heroism of her brother. When I picked up where she had left off, Germany had been reunited. The mayor was now more responsive. Later, Ul-rike Schrader, the director of the local Holocaust Memorial Cen-ter, made my cause her cause. With his party now in power in the nation's capital, Johannes Rau—soon to be elected president

Uncle Oswald Laufer, defender of the Weimar Republic, Social Democrat, and Reichsbanner; in 1933, he was assassinated by paramilitary Nazis in Elberfeld, Germany.

Wolfgang Ebert, leader of the local Social Democratic Party, the author, Johannes Rau, and Manfred at the unveiling of a plaque honoring Uncle Oswald, Wuppertal, 1998.

of Germany, longtime resident and onetime mayor of postwar Wuppertal, and Social Democratic prime minister of North Rhineland-Westphalia—participated in the ceremony honoring Oswald's memory. In 1998, on the sixty-fifth anniversary of Oswald's murder, Joshua (who bears Oswald's Hebrew name), Manfred, and I were formally invited to participate in a moving ceremony. Some fifty Social Democrats joined us in applause as the prime minister unveiled the plaque detailing Oswald's sacrifice as a Jew and a Reichsbanner.

When I was asked to speak, I recalled the terror that had taken the life of the young hero. However, I was really honoring his sister, our Mutti, and the triumphant New York Jewish life and attitudes she had ingrained in us despite her destroyed *Heimat* and battered emotions. I spoke in German except for the translation of "Shabbat Zachor," which this moment compelled me to pronounce in English:

Von meiner Kinderlehre: Da steht eine lange dunkele Mauer, an der linken Seite der langen Strasse. Da geh ich, Hand in Hand, mit Mutti, bis zum Jüdischen Friedhof. Und da steht sie, die liebe Mutter, und weint.

Am Grab des Bruders Yehoshua, Oswald Laufer, dort hat sie oft gestanden, in der Nazi Zeit, in den dreissiger Jahren, auch in 1940, das Jahr der Flüchtlingsreise nach Amerika.

Und noch einmal, nach dem Krieg. Damals stand sie, Schwester des Oswalds, und auch die Tochter der Eltern, dessen Tod kein Heimatsgrab in Wuppertal gefunden hat—nur Notizen in der Stadt, das man in Ghetto Lodz Necha und Schimon Laufer Tod gefunden hat.

Aber Mutti war auch Rosa Laufer Korman, selbständig, stolz, ein New Yorker: Mann und Kinder hatten den Holocaust überlebt, und der jüngste Bruder Sally war auch gesund und stark, verheiratet, und lebte mit Frau und Sohn Stephen in London.

Im Namen dieser Rosa Laufer, an diesem Tag, an diesem Shabbat Zachor, "this Shabbat of Remembrance," stehen wir alle—mein Bruder Manfred, mein Sohn Yehoshua, und durch uns fünf andere Kinder und fünfzehn Enkelkinder—stehen wir alle hier mit euch. Sie hatte immer die Hoffnung, immer geglaubt, dass ein Tag wie dieser ins Wuppertal kommen wird, ein Tag für Reichsbanner Oswald Laufer, Held der Weimarer Republik.

I gave Joshua and his siblings an English translation:

From my childhood: A long, dark wall on the left side of a street. I am walking, hand in hand with Mutti, into the Jewish cemetery. And there she stands, weeping.

At the grave of her brother Yehoshua, where she stood often, in Nazi days; also in 1940, when she fled to America.

And after the war. She stood, sister of Oswald, daughter of parents whose death brought no *Heimat*'s grave—only a town notice: Necha and Shimon Laufer died in Ghetto Lodz.

But Mutti was also Rosa Laufer Korman, independent, proud, a New Yorker. Husband and children outlived the Holocaust; so, too, her youngest brother Sally in London, at his side a wife and son, Stephen.

In the name of this Rosa Laufer, on this day, on this Shabbat Zachor, this Shabbat of Remembrance, we stand with you, all of us— my brother Manfred, my son Yehoshua, and through us five other children and fifteen grandchildren. She had always cherished the hope, always believed that into the Wupper valley this day would arrive for Reichsbanner Oswald Laufer, Hero of the Weimar Republic.

Together we had all returned to the 1930s, when the nightmare started.

Part II

Miss Cottage of Talaton

2

Everything changed that dark Friday morning when a policeman banged us awake and ordered us out of Germany. We panicked, protested, dressed, and packed, in ten minutes. Then he took us down the stairs, out the front door, down the stoop, up the street, and to the nearby police station, which just yesterday had protected Jews in the neighborhood. On this fateful October 28, 1938, we surrendered our only passport and joined shaken friends and acquaintances, some wearing prayer shawls and phylacteries. Around 9:30 A.M., as a small crowd jeered, we were driven away in open trucks. They stopped at a city jail. There Pappi was taken from us. We remained locked up the entire day, some thirty mothers and children listening to occasional screams from somewhere on the other side of the door. Around dusk guards returned to drive us from the prison. They stopped at Altona's Hauptbahnhof, one of metropolitan Hamburg's main railway stations—and yesterday's gateway to the beach.

The three of us—Mutti and her two little boys, aged six and ten—stood stock still, hand in hand and grasping a suitcase, overcome by panic and frightened at the sight of the long, black, belching train. Other Polish Jews had also been dumped at the station and were now looking for each other.[1] Where was he? There. No, that's not him. Look for two suitcases. "Pappi! Max! Pappi!" We and a thousand others screamed and screamed into the hall. When at last we found him, we had to board a guarded train and walk single file from car to car in order to look for seats and luggage space. Suddenly our family stopped the line for an instant: a second cousin stood in front of his seat, wine cup in hand, sanctifying the Shabbes for all of us.

31

Manfred, author, and Mutti in Hamburg, 1934-35.

Author at the beach in Hamburg's Blankenese, 1937–38.

In the next coach car we found seats next to windows facing the platform. "Push them down, down. Here, take the oranges," a stranger shouted from outside the compartment.[2] Hamburg's German Jews, free to come and go, had arrived with food and love. Our arms intertwined within the small space allowed us by the partially open windows. "Hurry. You are leaving," called the stranger.

The train rushed past station after station. Once, when it stopped, some of us somehow managed to get off the train long enough to give a platform official our postcards. At another station, on the long-deserted platform outside our windows, we saw a man walking, while on the other track another train arrived. It looked like ours. "Where are you from?" someone shouted. "Essen" came the reply. Then it left. Suddenly Mutti stretched her hand through the partially lowered window, waving a stamped envelope. The figure on the platform approached. She recognized him as one of those persons from the past, a reliable, polite employee of the German railway system. He came up to her. As he took the letter she pointed: "Please put it in that mailbox. My parents have to know where we are going." He smiled and said, "Of course." She replied: "Oh, thank you, thank you." As our train started to pull out of the station, he raised the envelope for her to see, tore it into shreds, and scattered it across the platform.

By dawn the ride was over. The sign on the station read "Neu Benschen." "It's the border, the border." Waiting soldiers lined us up on the open platform. We stood in the cold air. At the far end someone began shouting names. We heard "Korman" and felt Pappi leaving us. Another separation? Who called? Why? The soldier. An officer. Flared trousers in highly polished boots.

When Pappi returned holding his identity papers, I just knew that he could not tell me what to do next. After the last name rang out, a soldier's command made us turn right; by his command we started to walk. In his hands he held our hands even as we now held each other. But no matter what the next command. I knew we were supposed to be somewhere else: home in bed; planning activities for the morning; finding the Shabbes cake Mutti had baked and hidden on the upper shelf of her bedroom closet.

It was odd that my parents, who had tried to immigrate to the United States since 1936, had not anticipated some kind of action against themselves and other Polish Jews. It had not occurred to them to pack an emergency suitcase, like the ones pious ancestors had ready when the Messiah called. Far away from Neu Benschen, in the appropriate government ministries, a trail of paper about the likes of us—public documents used for cost analysis and record keeping—had already grown longer. Our deportation train was just one of many belonging to the Deutsche Reichsbahn, some of whose employees had shipped fifteen to eighteen thousand Polish Jews to various parts of the border country. The cost for the state was cheap. Calculated as a special passenger shipment, they had carried us at a minimum fee for a group of five hundred per train: 8.65 reichsmarks per person, a rate that was 40 percent of the full fare. The orders had come from the German government on October 6, when Poland announced a new passport rule: those of its citizens residing outside Poland for more than five years would lose their Polish citizenship if they did not return by October 30 to renew their passports.

The Nazi regime had moved quickly against traditional "outsiders," who in Germany had always been especially easy to pack and ship to the border. Following World War I, during newly independent Poland's wars and pogroms, Pappi had entered the Weimar republic from Polish Galicia by using the identity of his fallen soldier brother Osias Korman, settling in a town not far from Berlin. In 1927 he had married Rosa Laufer. Born in Germany, she and her two brothers were the children of Schimon and Necha Engelberg Laufer, Jews from Austria-Hungary who, in the midst of a migration of Polish workers into the industrial Ruhr at the turn of the century, had arrived in Elberfeld, a Prussian town famous for its textiles, monorail spanning the Wupper River, and for being the hometown of Friedrich Engels. According to the laws governing citizenship in central European countries, my brother Manfred and I, both born in Germany, were, like Mutti, assigned to a space under Pappi's Polish umbrella. Being a member of a Jewish family, since 1933 each of us had been subjected to all sorts of special Nazi laws and rules. These influenced every aspect of our lives. By the time of the deportation, we had been required to move into Hamburg's inner city, and in the months leading up to October Pappi had been forced out of his job. Still, until the thirtieth all of us were still Poles—or "Polish property," as Ernst von Weizaecker, state secretary of the

German Foreign Office, put it—including those who had been shipped from all over Germany to the eastern frontier, in particular to the Neu Benschen area. He told the Polish ambassador "that to accept Polish property—and that is what the Polish Jews are—does not seem to me such a great sacrifice."[3]

When we left our train and started a forced walk, we did not know that Neu Benschen was about seven kilometers from a frontier indicated by a gate and protected by Polish soldiers. We did know that Jews had walked like this before in the biblical Passover described in Exodus and in the Haggadah, which we had read at our seder table. As we thinned out, I pictured our long line in the prism of that ancient story. Mothers and fathers were carrying babies and toddlers or perching them on weary shoulders. Older children like us walked alongside our elders, each holding a pillow, a bag, or a suitcase. Men and women, some of whom were old, wearing all sorts of hats, were carrying or dragging bedding or just about anything else that might be useful in the unknown. Sometimes we saw farmers laughing as we walked past.

The threatening German soldiers marched alongside us until we saw a frontier gate being opened. Then they were positioned behind us. They were like Pharaoh's men, some arranged in an arc with rifles and fixed bayonets extended, others in flanking positions with hand-held machine guns at the ready. Unarmed, without protection from any government, we were in an open field facing Polish soldiers. "Stay back, stay back, against the bayonets. They will have to shoot over our heads. Stay out of the crossfire. Stay back, against the bayonets," Pappi commanded, his voice recalling his Austro-Hungarian military past.

In the distance, through the slowly moving crowd, we saw three Poles blocking our way. "There may be more in the trees, hiding," someone said as we heard their shots ring out, which forced each of us to hit the ground. "The suitcases, stand them up, in front of your faces. Lie down. Stay down," Pappi ordered quietly. We smothered the fall grass of this no-man's-land with our frightened Jewish bodies, Jewish property that no one wanted. There was no Red Sea to be parted.

But there was a leader, a heroic, anonymous figure lying in the first row, facing the three border guards. He displayed his

Zbaszyn, Poland, October 1938.

courage when he rose and ran into Poland. We followed him,
with the guns remaining silent, until, out of breath, we stumbled,
some almost into unconsciousness. Minutes passed, perhaps ten,
perhaps more. We waited for soldiers to force us back into the
field, but none came.

We were stateless refugees in the outskirts of Zbaszyn, a Polish
border town on the Berlin-Warsaw railway line. Its four thousand people, including six or seven Jewish families, had no idea
we were coming, yet somehow, almost twenty-seven hours after
the Hamburg policeman had come for us, word had reached
some enterprising locals with horse and wagon. I saw them coming down the country road without understanding their intentions. Pappi did. He said: "Don't give them the suitcases, don't.
We will never see our belongings again." But others did trust the
Poles; we saw full wagons departing down a road none of us
knew anything about.

When the Polish officers finally arrived, we followed them
along the same road the hustlers had taken, until we saw many
horses coming toward us. Their droppings guided us into three

dimly lit stables. Inside, we and another family Pappi had met when selling shoes in Hannover found a big straw bag on which to lie down. We were a few meters from the door, far from the other end of the dark stable where, during the evening, amid flashes of light, we heard the sound of ambulances and the cry of a newborn baby, held high for all to see.

Toward midnight someone spoke to us in Yiddish and German. These individuals, who worked for the American Jewish Joint Distribution Committee—we always called it the "Joint"—offered help and, later, sent reports and letters, some of which have survived. Within hours after we had been forced into Poland, they came from Warsaw. Three of them wrote to colleagues and friends about the "cruel and merciless" expulsion, which had brought them and us to Zbaszyn. One was historian Emanuel Ringelblum, who now had his first experience of Nazi brutality. He was stunned by what he saw: "A woman, still half-crazed . . . evicted from her home in Germany, still in her pajamas. Another woman, approximately fifty years old . . . paralyzed and carried out of her house to the border on an armchair held by young Jewish men. A man suffering from sleeping sickness . . . carried across the border on a stretcher." When, on December 6, 1938, he wrote about these acts to Raphael Mahler, a distinguished fellow historian, Ringelblum told him that despite the "very cold" weather many of us still had to wait "for a long time before being served [a noonday meal]. . . . People still feel they are in a large camp. For the past five weeks, people have slept on straw mats in large dormitories. Although the halls are heated, there is no possibility to change clothes. The 'public bath' has raised its price to 50 zlotys [approx. fifteen dollars] per bath and not everyone can bathe." Ringelblum also wrote Mahler:

I do not think any Jewish community has ever experienced so cruel and merciless an expulsion as this one. . . . The [Polish] government is not giving us a cent. We paid in full for straw we received during the first days from the district government. . . . People in the camp have received notices that they have lost their Polish citizenship. . . . This camp will become a propaganda vehicle; and no Jew will be allowed into Poland. We Poles are the true antisemites. We will evacuate Zbaszyn only when the internees have the possibility of immigration. Zbaszyn has become the symbol for the defenselessness of

Polish Jews. Jews have been humiliated to the level of lepers, to fourth-class citizens, and as a result we are all affected by this terrible tragedy.

By the time he wrote his letter, Kristallnacht had occurred on November 9–10. Before being killed in Warsaw's general uprising in 1944, Ringelblum documented earlier horrors in the Warsaw Ghetto. In his historical accounts, Zbaszyn was a harbinger of coming terror and thus became one more deportation and refugee dump, different from but yet comparable to earlier ones, before there had been a Nazi state. From our own perspective, Zbaszyn was *the* unprecedented Polish Jewish tragedy described by Ringelblum.

There are other letters that described our plight ("thousands . . . sheltered in the so-called barracks, horse stables, 10 men in every box"). Most of us tried to stay outside—even as late as 3 A.M. Many needed medical attention, including over a hundred

Zbaszyn, Poland, October 1938.

already in nearby hospitals. Two thousand who had money for railway fares left in the first two days—one by throwing himself in front of a train. The Poles added to the mood of despair: the thousand or so who paid twenty-five thousand zlotys for a rail ticket into the interior were told to board and find seats only to be ordered back to the barracks.[4]

At dawn of our second day in the stables Mutti was gone. Pappi said, "to the railway station," to hide from the Poles, who wanted to send her back because she was not born in Poland. When she returned the following day, she reported that she had avoided Polish officials by always moving about among the crowds in and around the small train station. In the meanwhile, we had learned how to make good use of a "pot" that had somehow appeared on our straw sack. We peed, washed, and boiled water in it, but I do not remember where we defecated or how we got the water or lit the fire.

That morning we and others milled around some of the food trucks that had just arrived. They were bringing bread and butter and eggs, from on high. We formed two lines. First, I stood on one line for bread and butter while watching two figures bending, straightening, and then throwing something over the side. When my turn came, I saw how one bent down to get the bread, breaking it by hitting it against the side of the truck, while the other slapped a slice of butter on the part of the loaf that the first was now throwing over the side, all the time expecting me to catch both before either bread or butter hit the ground. Then I tried to catch the eggs.

A while later our family rushed to a line to buy spaces in automobiles that were to take us into the interior of Poland. Perhaps we would finally meet Pappi's parents, a brother, cousins, all of whom lived in one house. He had remained in touch, indeed, had sent packages of clothing plus a 1936 photo showing my first day in first grade. Pappi had sometimes visited them, but he always did so alone. They all lived in Narol, just outside Lemberg. Then I did not know of my grandfather's remarkable reputation among the Belzer Hasidim, against whose devout ways his youngest son, my father, had rebelled. In fact, Manfred and I were the grandsons of Haskel Maites! Among the Kormans and those who knew him, that was considered *yichus,* an honored lineage.

Except for my Aunt Resi, another rebel who had lived with us in Hamburg for one year before moving to Palestine, I knew little about Pappi's family—his mother, Leah; my uncle Wolf and his wife, Dvora; another aunt also named Dvora, who with her husband, Wolf Bottwin, had gone to Argentina—and literally nothing about the many first and second cousins from Narol and neighboring towns and villages.[5] However, in 1938 there would be no meeting with any of them. While others bought seats and left for Cracow, Warsaw, Posen, Lodz, or Lemberg, we, who did not have their kind of money, left the line with our three suitcases to face the next uncertain hour.

We had little control. Anything could happen. On the third day we separated. Somehow Pappi had found floor space in the home of one of the religious Jewish families in Zbaszyn. Along with four or five other boys, Manfred and I slept on bare wooden floors, huddled under a thin blanket or two. We ate as before, near the trucks outside the stable, or perhaps at the relief station set up by the Joint. Pappi and Mutti ate elsewhere.

In Zbaszyn there were no assets to convert into cash. Not that Pappi and Mutti had much to begin with: an old Ford, furniture, clothing, toys, some household silver, and a savings account containing roughly 850 reichsmarks. They did not own an apartment, a house, or land—Pappi had been a shoe salesman and had earned a modest living. What they had left behind was put in the care of a Hamburg attorney to whom, fortuitously, Pappi had assigned power of attorney a couple of days before the deportation in order to deal with tax claims. Between Zbaszyn and Hamburg the two stayed in touch by letter and postcard, obeying the rules and regulations of the Third Reich. With the help of relatives and Mutti's father in Elberfeld, the Ford was sold for 125 reichsmarks. Some of Pappi's former employers still owed him money, but these amounts could not be collected since one of them had also been deported. The household belongings were placed in sealed storage, ostensibly to be forwarded or taken to a different country of residence. That "service" cost 15 reichsmarks a month. Even though Pappi, who was renamed "Israel Osias Korman" by Nazi officials, had been denied all work opportunities since the beginning of 1938, the tax collector demanded the 70 reichsmarks owed him. Even the landlord succeeded in

Pappi in Zbaszyn, Poland, 1938–39.

collecting his monthly rent of 280 reichsmarks until February 1939. Everything was duly documented, duplicated, authenticated, and filed with the Office of Foreign Exchange Control![6]

By the end November, life in Zbaszyn acquired some degree of regularity. Pappi remained outside of assigned housing. Freer than we were to move about, he had managed to rent space from the same family whose floor we had shared, while the rest of us went to one of the buildings the Joint acquired: a six-story abandoned flour mill. That's what we understood it to be when we moved in and tried to cope with its cold walls and cement floors. Although there were rough wooden bed frames—each with straw mattress, sheet, and scratchy blanket—we three and some others had to settle for a couple of blankets and two straw sacks on the floor, which remained cold even at midday. Our nights were communal; men, women, children, and babies all slept together. Who undressed?

Here Mutti, now a tigress, took charge. A reserved Jewish middle-class wife and mother, she soon realized that her married life had been shattered by this expulsion, which, in the perspective of Zbaszyn, had been foreshadowed five years earlier with the political murder of her heroic brother, Oswald Laufer. In Elberfeld, during the last years of the Weimar republic, he had become a local leader of the militant anti-Nazi Reichsbanner. The Nazis, in turn, marked him as one of their leading public enemies. In early 1933, the day before Purim and amid Nazi electoral victory celebrations in Elberfeld, they brutally assassinated him in front of his parents' house.[7] Aged twenty-seven, his parents buried him in the Jewish cemetery where Mutti would bring me to honor his memory.

Mutti had reared us because Pappi, a traveling salesman for German shoe firms, was usually away for weeks on end, including many a Sabbath. She was simply following the circumscribed yet generally accepted rules of conduct in a traditional East European Jewish family. Now, however, she was a different sort of mother. In the mill her husband no longer set the rules; others did, and for her sons' well-being she had decided to become one of those others. Even though it meant rising earlier than everyone else in Zbaszyn's winter dawn, in one of the coldest parts of

Mutti in Zbaszyn, Poland, 1938–39.

the mill she spent hours preparing sandwiches for the mill's five hundred deportees: her children would have their morning glass of tea plus bread and butter, or, later, just bread and jam. No one ever tried to take bread away from her, even when raw violence flared at mealtimes as hungry, cold, scared refugees fought over an extra slice of bread, hot soup, potatoes, or, for a while, meat when it was served as part of the main noontime dinner. No wonder I remember eating only Mutti's bread and butter in Zbaszyn.

We were living in a makeshift Jewish town, a refugee camp; but we did have important emotional and religious havens about which Ringelblum also wrote. "There are organized discussions of Zionist youth. . . . On Saturday songs have been heard in the barracks. A confirmation had been celebrated and the Torah was read. . . . . Vast cultural activities have developed," including the use of Yiddish, which he thought "has become the vogue of the camp." Besides classes in Polish, he and others also set up "several reading rooms and a library." Religious groups, he reported, "have set up a Talmud Torah school," while music lovers have their concerts and also "an active choir."[8]

I remember falling in love with Yiddish, but, even more important, embracing the Zionist youth movement, which celebrated Shabbes every Friday night on the fifth floor—nicknamed the Zionist floor—of our mill. This small group of deported pioneers wrapped me in their stories and dreams and draped me in their protective shawl, which shielded me from the humiliation and despair all around me. I might be forced to walk alone, cut off from loved ones by police and soldiers, abandoned by all who were not Jews. Hamburg and Zbaszyn had turned on me. I knew what "they" were thinking: the Germans deported us, so the family Grinspan is also here, in the mill where Mutti met them. Their son in Paris went wild when he heard what had happened. In an act of revenge he tried to assassinate Ernst von Rath in the German embassy. So the Germans unleashed Kristallnacht. Who knew what the Poles would do to the Grinspans and all those who had come in contact with them.

I consciously embraced Zionism as if my very life depended on it, a boy from the Neu Benschen platform, commanded by a German soldier, forced to accept new feelings of self-reliance.

Zionism was familiar, known to Pappi for many years. Its collective ideology was portable—and I was on the move. In Germany I had belonged to Brith Hanoar, a Zionist youth movement, and to Maccabi, the Zionist sports organization that also accepted members under ten years of age. However, the Zbaszyn Zionism of the mill's fifth floor was different! Even at ten I knew that no matter what fate awaited our tiny family of four, Zionism's protective shawl would always renew my hope that one day Jews in Palestine would manage everything by themselves.

3

Within the established boundaries of our refugee camp, my enterprising Pappi managed to bring us together in Nadnia. Sometime before spring arrived he had rented a one-room cottage next to a farmhouse on a sandy lane leading to a lake, which at its northern edge skirted Zbaszyn. Compared to the stable and mill, these beachlike accommodations were luxurious; compared to Hamburg, Nadnia, with its dirt tracks and handful of cobblestone-paved streets, caused our wooden shoes—which we now wore to protect our leather ones from mud and rain—to elicit primitive sounds. But we made do with what we had and shared our space and food with those in need; on a warm day that may have been no more than homemade drinks—a lemonade or a concoction that included bicarbonate of soda, water, and jelly. I learned how to chop wood and milk goats like the residents of Nadnia. We could have bought meat from our new landlord, who slaughtered his own pigs, but kosher laws made us dependent on the local Jewish butcher of Zbaszyn. We made regular visits to the Joint's general store, sometimes hitching rides on the haywagons of local farmers but usually on foot. On such occasions we would pass Polish youngsters, who almost always cursed us for being Jews. That's how we learned their slurs "kiss my ass," and "catch the cholera Jew." But they never hit us.

If Mutti showed her aggressive side in the flour mill, Pappi now demonstrated his passion for organized Jewry. He decided there were enough Jews in Nadnia to establish a congregation and a satellite store. I had known him only as a member of a big-city congregation where others did the moving and shaking. Here in Nadnia he was a mover. It was with pride that I walked alongside him that day, the cobblestones wet and slippery, to some house where, in a room furnished with religious objects and prayer books, he and I worshiped together for the first time since we had been imprisoned in Zbaszyn. Manfred and Mutti were not with us, probably because that Sabbath Manfred was still recovering from a whooping cough that had dragged on for many weeks. We were fortunate that his was the only serious illness among the four of us.

Being sick in Zbaszyn was especially dangerous. Others had already suffered catastrophes, like the family of Yossel Kamiel. I had met him on one of our visits to the Joint's store. Its high shelves seemed to surround a desk and register of some sort. Instead of a ladder, the manager stood on his toes to reach sacks of flour just above shoulder height. Beyond that he had help from an ever so nimble Yossel, a boy about as old as Manfred. He scrambled from shelf to shelf, awaiting orders from the manager to throw this or that bag into waiting arms below. I recall thinking that was all he ever saw: arms attached to hands poised to catch the item. I remembered him. It was his father who had died of an unanticipated asthma attack.

Manfred, whom the deportation experience had already tagged with a pronounced stutter, spent the last of his sick days in our room. When the weather turned warmer, he rested near the waterfront, which we had all but ignored. Now, in the weeks before Passover, two of our neighbors introduced us to offshore fishing.

The two brothers were twins, fully grown men a little taller than my short parents, with dark, curly hair and eyeglasses to match. Having decided to imitate local fishermen, they cut down branches, trimmed them, fashioned a hook from safety pins, dug for worms, and found string among their belongings. One warm afternoon Manfred and I spotted them at the end of our lane, near the edge of the lake. They stood behind each other, the one a few steps from us watching his brother, who, in turn, was watching the fisherman casting his line on the beach. Every once in a while he brought the stick over his shoulder and sent the string and hook toward us in a swishing motion before they reentered the lake. Suddenly the fisherman caught his twin brother's lip. He screamed, fell into the sand, and turned and twisted as his brother tried to remove the hook.

Following this incident, our families decided to celebrate Pass-over together. They had more space, so in preparation for the seder we brought some of our furnishings to them. Except for fresh vegetables, which we could purchase from local farmers, and chickens from the kosher butcher, the Passover food must have come from the general store. Somehow by late afternoon everything was under control: Manfred and I were walking to the home of the twins, rehearsing the traditional four questions along the way. The injured twin was also ready.

Each of our two seders followed traditional Orthodox Jewish ritual—our parents would not have done it any other way. No matter how they observed or failed to observe religious rules of conduct for everyday living, the Sabbath, or other Jewish holi-days, Passover, the celebration of Jewish freedom, was a special event that simply had to be honored and celebrated in traditional ways. Whatever circumstances refugee life on the Polish border had imposed, each of the seders as well as the rest of Passover had to be properly conducted.

We kept still about Pappi's departure for Germany. On the third day of Passover he left from the railway station where Mutti had hidden from Polish officials. Together with other for-mer heads of households, he was returning to Hamburg with the permission of a German government that was trying to use the deportees to straighten out the legal and financial mess the de-portation had caused within local governments and the courts. At his own expense, in three weeks he was expected to close all open accounts and resolve all outstanding legal obligations. We also hoped that before returning to Zbaszyn he might be able to get us out—perhaps to America—by contacting an old friend here or a former contact there.[1]

So now it was "Auf Wiedersehen." As Pappi stood behind the moving open compartment window, both arms stretched toward us, hands waving up and down, we sensed it was good-bye for a long time to come. In teary silence we turned away from the rail-road crossing so that we could no longer see the train rushing back to Germany.

It need not have happened, this painful separation in a mood of fear. Since 1936 my parents had been desperately trying to get all of us to the United States. By the time of the deportation, all kinds of obstacles had stood in the way, some intentionally placed there by the U.S. State Department—whose embassies and consular agencies in those depression years were riddled with nativism, antisemitism, and corruption—and some created by American relatives, who, according to Mutti, feared that the niece of their rich father would compete for his money. Finally, in July 1938, when we had the necessary affidavits to register with the consul in Hamburg, Pappi and Mutti received different numbers on two waiting lists: 1,124–25 on the Polish one because he had been born in Poland; and 4,380 on the German one because Mutti, Manfred, and I had been born in Germany. Since the American quota for migrants from Poland was exhausted, only those of German birth were asked to report to the consulate on February 10, 1939. By then, however, the deportation had made it impossible for us to appear. Besides, our files had been sent to the appropriate American immigration officials in Warsaw. (After more than two months, in response to Pappi's inquiries, that consul replied with a form letter announcing that we would have to wait a few years for our turn to apply for visas.) While in Hamburg, Pappi had contacted consular officials who agreed that the number assigned to his wife and children on the German quota was the valid one. However, he was also told that Hamburg officials had no influence at all with those in Warsaw. That news meant that my parents had to turn to Jewish agencies in order to overcome the obstacles American and European officials were putting in the way of Jews trying to reach the United States.

In April 1939 Pappi's most important contact in the United States was Selma W. Basker, executive director of Service to the Foreign Born, an agency of the National Council of Jewish Women in Miami, Florida. It was her office that had finally contacted Mutti's uncle in Miami, successfully working around obstructionist relatives, and had arranged for affidavits.[2] Pappi pleaded with Mrs. Basker to somehow intervene with American officials in Warsaw and in Washington, D.C. Why had the Hamburg gateway to the United States been slammed shut? He had tried to deal with Warsaw, but the latter took nine or ten weeks to respond—with form letters. There was no point in sending the files back to Hamburg because an invitation to the American consul did not elicit permission from the German government to cross the frontier. He pleaded with her: at least get my family out of the "Zbaszyn swamp."[3]

Within days after he had waved to us at the Zbaszyn station, Pappi found another way to get all of us out of Zbaszyn—or at least that's what he thought at the time. In the same three weeks of Hamburg residence granted him, the Hamburg-America (Hapag) steamship *St. Louis* was scheduled to transport some nine hundred Jews from Hamburg to Havana, Cuba. If he could get on board and land in Cuba, which had a privileged position in American immigration law, he'd be able to enter the United States within a year and then bring the three of us to America. Christian Geissler, an old friend and neighbor who in 1939 was still an official with the Hapag, made it possible for Pappi to get a ticket when Baruch Weissman, another friend who had recently immigrated to Cuba, managed to purchase a landing permit from a senior Cuban immigration official. The transaction for this extraordinary opportunity to leave Europe cost Pappi $150, the fee Weissman paid to a local Havana attorney.

Years later, when Pappi wrote a few lines about his *St. Louis* voyage, he recalled Christian Geisler, for he had always greatly appreciated what his neighbor had done. In 1939 he had saved his life; a year later, by "certifying her a passage in the Hapag for the United states," he had saved Mutti's life as well. "Without it she would have been deported to Poland or put into a concentration camp."[4]

Even though Pappi's departure for Havana justified our worst fears after he had left Zbaszyn, the news of his sailing was just another of those events that made little impact on me at the time. He was gone, and that was that. Hopefully everything would work itself out—but it wouldn't. He was gone, out of Zbaszyn, out of sight. Who could predict what would happen? When his letter containing news about the voyage arrived, I was ready. Everything was spelled out in black and white: according to Zbaszyn's Zionists, there were no shades of gray in living nightmares.

"Exactly at eight in the evening," he wrote, "as the ship began to move slowly from its moorings, a grand vision possessed each of us: sixteen days in a luxurious floating hotel; sixteen days of freedom from burdens and sorrow; sixteen days to be climaxed in Havana by the embrace of loved ones, by the chance to send for wives and children, and parents who remained behind. A new chapter was to begin for us all."[5]

It was a naive expectation, for the voyage turned into a cruel hoax that benefited the German government. With the annexation of Austria and Czechoslovakia, the deportations to Poland, and then Kristallnacht, the Nazi regime had publicly demonstrated its escalating anti-Jewish terror policies and had proclaimed that the rest of the world also did not want Jews. The *St. Louis* had left Hamburg a week after the Cuban government, without compensation, had voided all those landing permits purchased for thousands of dollars by Pappi and hundreds of others. (In Havana rumor had it that some six thousand permits had been sold.) However, Hapag assured the passengers that the void decree did not apply to the permits because that decree had been issued after the landing permits had already been granted. In fact, in the spring preceding the German invasion of Poland, Pappi and the other *St. Louis* passengers had become 936 more Jewish boat people wandering across the Atlantic Ocean, the Black Sea, or the Mediterranean.

The ship arrived in Havana waters two days early, on a Saturday. At 4 A.M. that morning those who were awake could see the lights of the city. The *St. Louis* had dropped anchor and soon procedures for leaving the vessel were under way. Pappi described what happened next: "Everything became quiet. Then we saw a decree from the Cuban police, but at first we did not know what it meant." All sorts of rumors now circulated: Cubans did not work on the Saturday before Pentecost, they had arrived too early and had to wait their turn as other ships in the harbor unloaded. Then relatives and friends arrived on small motorboats and shouted "mañana, mañana" at them as they stood at the railing. After a day or so, the passengers lost patience and returned the "mañana, mañana" calls in a mood of desperation. "Finally, we did not even want to see the boats. . . . [We] cursed and wept. Many broke down. . . . On Thursday we heard that the ship would have to leave harbor early Friday morning. . . . [We] organized [our] young people to stand uninterrupted two-hour watches to prevent . . . suicides."

The balance of his letter graphically revealed the truth about our lonely, precarious Jewish lives:

The ship turned, and slowly, very slowly, left the port, accompanied by the many small boats, and also by autos driving along the harbor front. . . . At first, when the ship stopped after a few hours of travel, all sighed with relief: the coast of Havana was still in view. But then, even as the first dispatches came, imploring us to be courageous and patient, the *St. Louis* suddenly resumed its journey at full speed. The next morning, seemingly moving toward Cuba, we found ourselves looking at the coast of Florida: Miami's skyscrapers, beaches, the bridge to Key West. All these wonderful facilities seemed within a swimmer's reach. As the yachts and other luxury boats greeted us, you can well imagine the feeling that dominated me. Here lived our uncle [who had sent affidavits for each of us]; this was the land to which I was supposed to come. And here I was so near, but oh so far.

When it seemed certain that the liner would have to return to Germany, Pappi exploded, his cherished central European Enlightenment values now shattered:

What rotten merchandise Jews must be if no one is prepared to accept us. The slaves must have been better: at least people paid for them, but here and now, when many wanted to pay for each of us, we are still rejected. Are we really so bad and rotten? Are we really humanity's vermin and thus to be treated as lepers? Or has mankind ceased being human? Has it decided to imitate the natural elements and join with them in a war of annihilation against all the weaker and helpless forms of life? If yes, then man stands revealed. You have no capacity for understanding. You have no ideals. You have no noble purpose. Man, you are lower than the beasts. They fight only when driven by hunger, by nature's survival demands, which leave them no choice. You, man, use your ability to reason, to kill, to destroy. And what a hero you are, man. You battle against the weakest. Among your kind are great scientists: they specialize in studying the most complex, difficult problems. You do everything to help them because you claim that their research will yield the best of all possible results for your kind. But with us Jews, man, you preach one thing and practice the opposite: you destroy what you do not comprehend or do not want to comprehend. Man, you are a lie.[6]

The oceanic wanderings, however, did not end in Germany. Instead, a dramatic intervention facilitated by the Joint brought the ship to Antwerp, Belgium, where he was assigned to the 181-passenger contingent that was sent in a small boat to Rotterdam, in Holland; the others were sent to England and France or remained in Belgium. Years later we learned that friends from Hamburg, who had immigrated to England, sent two letters to Antwerp in which they presented themselves as sponsors for two passengers, one for a nephew, the other for Pappi. The nephew was sent to England. The letter for Pappi had arrived too late—perhaps.

Joseph Harsch, an American journalist, reported on the selection: The English "skimmed off the cream at the outset." The French refused "any Poles at all. . . . No one wanted the 'Statenlos' [stateless], and equally avoided those with no evidence of prospects in the United States. . . . The Belgians and the Dutch in particular felt that things were not going as planned or in accordance with the original agreement that each country would accept a proportion of the undesirables. The upshot was that in the end neither Belgian nor Dutch took the original agreed quotas. The British, having had first choice, were forced, most reluctantly, to accept the final residue of undesirables to a total of 287."[7]

Unaware of most of these details until the mail arrived later in June, Mutti took charge, trying to cope with the world in which she and her children had to manage by themselves. First we moved into a small apartment in Zbaszyn proper, near the soccer stadium. Then she looked for ways to get her children out of Poland and herself back on the road to the United States.

She decided to split the family once more, risking the possibility that she would never see us again. In order to get her sons out of Poland, she was prepared to have us join a Zionist Youth Aliya group headed for Palestine while she went back to Hamburg for her own and her children's visas. We took a train to Poznan, a short distance from Zbaszyn, initiated immigration procedures, returned on the same day, and then waited for news about our departure. It never happened. Upon hearing that we were on a children's transport list bound for London, Mutti chose the road to England as the best way out.[8]

She made her choice from among alternatives provided by transport organizers working diligently with government officials, who steadfastly refused to admit the children's Jewish parents. These private efforts, usually funded with Joint money raised from relatives of victims and from other contributors, sought to connect Jewish children from the Continent with Jewish host families or organizations, many of whom were in England. By the spring of 1939 one of the uncommon Kindertransport journeys was supposed to start from Otwock, a small town near Warsaw, and then go from the Polish capital, via Gdinya on the Baltic, to Southampton, England. There the children were supposed to go by train to London, to the Jewish families who had promised to house and feed them for the duration of the emergency. This was the transport Mutti chose, acting on an initiative started by Pappi. While in Hamburg, he had contacted the Federation of Polish Jews in England. This organization had been prepared to add our names to an already long list of children looking for connections to British Jewish families.[9]

We had been lucky. For a brief moment in June 1939, in Zbaszyn on the German frontier, two small children foolishly believed that Mutti would be able to retrieve us on her way to the United States. I heard the news while playing in the stadium and ran home to announce it. Preparations for our departure began almost immediately, with ongoing battles against lice. Manfred turned ours into a memorable occasion by successfully hiding from everyone for a few hours. I thought he would be happy to go, but to my surprise he started to cry and hid from Mutti in a haystack. Perhaps he cried because he hated to be scrubbed in the tub, was afraid of the barber, loved his hair, or had panicked at the sight of other children with short hair.

Perhaps he was really hiding and crying because he was being forced to endure the unimaginable act of leaving his mother so soon after having seen his father go. He was seven and a half years old and I was a few weeks from my eleventh birthday; that is, he was five out of diapers and I five into literacy when it was Mutti's turn to push us away. On the Neu Benschen platform soldiers had stripped Pappi of his authority. Now it was her turn to push us out and adopt personalities of our own choosing. We had completed potty training for daytime hours and I had accepted the family's middle-class conventions concerning daily conduct and ritual observance, especially in such extreme circumstances determined by martial law. Somehow we would have to manage, to cut our losses and make do with what we had, in trains or boats or trucks or in other shelters along the way to nowhere and everywhere.

4

Sometime in June we and others in the "transport" left from the same train station where we had waved good-bye to Pappi. This time it was five in the evening and the weather was hot. Manfred and I were dressed in custom-tailored white linen suits, which Mutti had somehow managed to have made in Zbaszyn. It had been a bribe to persuade Manfred to come out of a tree and join the transport. Amid the tumult, at 5:45 P.M., the train pulled in amid a cloud of steam: "Auf Wiedersehen, Bubi! Take care of him. Manfred, listen to him! Write! Oh, dear God!" And then it was as if the station wept, for the children were leaving. We were at the open window, arms outstretched and waving both hands toward our weeping Mutti. We passed by slowly, numbed by the noisy train as it sped from her.

I was in charge. There surely must have been a chaperone to make all the connections in Warsaw so that we would end up in a place called Otwock, where we would meet our Kindertransport bound for England. No matter. I felt in charge. Of course, I had no idea what would happen next; nor could I have done much about it: I was a third-class veteran, a Zbaszyn traveler, a bed wetter, stateless, frightened by government officials and expecting the worst to happen. I could not speak Polish, but with absurd confidence I assumed I'd manage with my German, newly learned Germanized Yiddish, and with the few phrases I had learned in English at my Talmud Torah parochial school in Hamburg. I did have the heavens where the night sky's stars and moon were on guard, listening for the shrill whistle of our engine, making certain we were heading in the right direction. Meanwhile our beds needed tending. After lining up matching suitcases on the floor for Manfred to sleep on, I squeezed into the wooden bench of the compartment.

We slept until breakfast time. Around six I got up, washed, roused Manfred, and then went off to find food and some of the other Zbaszyn children. The train was still in open country, but we were near Lodz. Sometime later the train pulled into the great railway station of Warsaw. Someone did instruct us to take a bus to an Otwock youth hostel belonging to the Organization for Rehabilitation and Training (ORT), an organization that provided vocational training for orphans and other Jewish youngsters. We were told to drop our suitcases in front of one of the shacks and to go into the dining hall for lunch, which consisted of fried eggs and bread. There we met the man in charge, who told us that all the boys and girls of the transport would have to stay in Otwock for a while. There were not yet enough English Jewish families to take all of us. Right! Lunch over, we were assigned to bunks, told to unpack, and instructed to write postcards to our parents telling them of our journey and safe arrival.

Being a former overnight camper with experience of summer camp in the German resort town of Bad Kissingen, in my eyes our place in Otwock was, well, a dump. We had "brand-new bedding when we arrived, but they were never changed during our whole stay," I wrote in a notebook shortly afterward. "The food was good the first two days, but then it began getting worse and worse. It became so bad that we hated mealtime. . . . Whenever we had good food, which was very seldom, we got so little that we left the dining hall hungry. . . . When there was bad food, we got so much of it that ¾ of it had to be thrown [out] because nobody touched it. They tried to stuff it down our throats by making speeches and promises. It really became terrible. I had some money for the camp canteen, but it soon ran out." Manfred and I received three zlotys in a food package sent by a relative who lived in Poland, and that helped briefly. We also had our soccer. There were enough boys to organize two teams, which competed for the honor of camp champion.

Despite our complaints to Mutti, we had no choice but to wait with everyone else. But when Mutti wrote that she was leaving for Germany in order to get to the United States, I informed the head of the camp that both our parents had left Poland.

At the time I did not realize what Pappi and Mutti were up against. Each had to cope with consulates, public-security officials, and refugee committees; and both were desperate when they learned we were stuck in Poland. In July 1939, while still in Rotterdam, the Amsterdam-based Committee for Special Jewish Matters asked Pappi to pay for his upkeep. It was the first in a series of letters from Amsterdam and Miami raising support questions, travel expenses, and the like, forcing him to respond that they should use every penny in the multiple accounts under the family name to get his wife and children out of Europe.[1] In the case of the Amsterdam committee, he had to reply: "I left Hamburg with four dollars and these I have spent. Unfortunately I have no resources abroad. Also my relatives cannot help me. I therefore take the liberty of returning your bill."[2]

As the threat of war loomed, the American consulate in Hamburg in effect forced Pappi to sign his own death warrant. Registered under the Polish quota, he was asked to agree to let his wife and children emigrate without him.[3] He was also beside himself when he learned from us in mid-August that the transport was still in Otwock. He wrote to the Polish Refugee Fund in London: "A fourteen-day delay in these precarious conditions is a very long time. What should such little children do alone and abandoned? Have they not endured enough? The deportation and the journey to Zbaszyn and the life there itself. Now they are all alone, hoping day after day to finally reach England, and they are again disappointed. . . . After the wild ride of the 'St. Louis' I am here, my wife is in Hamburg, and the children insecure in Poland. Our longing, our hope is . . . to know that the children are safe. Please. At least fulfill that hope."[4]

On August 23, 1939, Mutti, still in Hamburg, discovered that her immigration papers were not yet in order. Officially identified as a Polish national, she had managed to obtain the required immigration documents from Polish officials. Now the American consular officials wrote that her uncle needed to open a bank account in her name. He was, after all, a man of seventy-two who could die at any moment, possibly even during the first year of Mutti's arrival in the United States. The American government had to have a year's guarantee that his niece and her children would not become wards of the state while she was looking for work. At the very least, he had to provide seventy-five dollars a month. She wrote Pappi: "I am going to send the original [letter from the consulate] to Mrs. Basker and hope you can at once contact the uncle. At first the Consul demanded the uncle promise he would take care of us. Now he demands a bank account. Always something else. . . . Perhaps you can also write to Mrs. Basker. Hopefully the uncle will do this. . . . With God's help the children will sail in a good hour."[5]

Meanwhile we were in camp, enjoying life as best we could. During a brief stay in the infirmary, I awoke one morning to find a moving black bedcover. Ever so gently I removed my belt from the pair of trousers lying on the chair nearby, uncoiled it, and lifted it high above the bed. Then, in a series of swift strokes, I massacred one long line of flies after another until the moving black bedcover lay still.

Tomatoes were a standard part of our diet, but after one meal the rotten ones initiated a camp scene of their own. Boys and girls slept in different bunks. Manfred and I slept in one where perhaps as many twenty were housed under one roof, surrounded by torn wire screens pretending to guard against flies and mosquitoes. After we had been in bed for a while, each of us rushed to the screens, turned around, and placed our bare behinds against the mesh, laughing all the while. Expelled by the force of the tomatoes, the evening meal rushed to the ground below, never once allowing us to consider the outhouses and their millions of worms.

On August 20, a Wednesday, rumors about our departure from Otwock began to circulate—details tomorrow, after breakfast. That morning a hundred or so anxious children who had hardly touched their food sat at the dining hall's long tables, now cleared of dishes and cutlery. Manfred was at the opposite end of the room from where I sat. We fell silent when the director commanded us to keep quiet and talked about the list he was about to read. I heard something like "and some of you will not be on this list . . . will have to remain behind. We cannot wait any longer for the Jewish families who have not yet come forward." He started to read our names. I heard mine almost at once, but Manfred's did not follow. Then, near the end of the list, he read his name. We jumped onto the tables, ran toward each other, and embraced, relieved yet in tears for the ones who had to stay behind.

(Many years afterwards I learned about certain congressmen who opposed our coming to the United States, claiming that we would join the ranks of the unemployed during the Great Depression, that we were potential thieves who would steal work from starving sharecropper children.)

Soon we packed and played. A few years later I wrote about our departure. "Going into Manfred's bunk, I told him to take [his clothing] into my bunk so we could pack together as we had just one suitcase. All our clothe were clean, although they were very creased as they had never been ironed. We had to wash our own clothe as there was no laundry around. It took us about two hours to pack all our clothe neatly. At half past three we went out in the yard to play volleyball as they had taken our soccer ball away."

There were yet other preparations. On Sunday morning, August 24, the day we were to leave, Manfred told me, "They're examining heads for lice." We had been through that experience before, so although I was certain we had done everything to remain clean, I knew that "in this filth anything was liable to happen"—and it did. This time the procedure was different. When my turn came, I was surprised that our heads had to be washed.

Then the nurse [examined] the hair with a steel comb. Twice the hard steel comb went through my hair. . . . I looked on the comb and there, crawling along, was a louse. I bit my lip and tears came into my eyes. It hurts a lot when you try to be clean all your life and then because of dirty and disgusting beds your hair becomes a nest for lice. Manfred had better luck: by him they pulled out two lice. What could you do? Nothing, nothing at all except wash your hair with a certain chemical. After getting through with that, it was about half past eight, and at this time we heard we were going to lose our hair. First we didn't believe it, but when we saw one of our friends shaved to the skin our hearts fell. . . . Some of us tried to hide, but it was no use—every one of us was caught.

When my turn came, I used my pocket mirror to watch the barber do his dirty work. He "took out his shears and over my head it went. First the left side . . . then the middle and at last the right side." What would the English think, I wondered, about boys with shaved heads?

We left in a panic. After the haircuts, we had to take the beds out of the bunk and place them in a shed to air them out, "those beds which had caused so much trouble to all of us. It was a terrible feeling. . . . As soon as we had done our share, we scrubbed our hands thoroughly to prevent another attack of our little enemies." Suddenly one of our boys came running with a newspaper in hand. He screamed: "Poland is mobilizing. The cruiser *Königsberg* is coming." We continued our chores. The staff was frazzled. The lines to Warsaw and Gdinya were jammed. After about an hour, around 9:30 A.M., we assembled in the dining hall to get our marching orders from the camp's tense director. He confirmed the names on the departure list, reminded us of the urgency of the moment, and sent us out of the dining hall. Rickety buses drove us from Otwock to the Warsaw railway station.[6]

It was sheer bedlam on this first day of Poland's mobilization. Civilian trains were being converted into troop carriers. Together with armed soldiers, we boarded the train to Gdinya while many officials, friends, and relatives milled about on the platform. The atmosphere was chaotic for another reason, since many parents had heard about our transport and were trying desperately to put their children on the train during these frantic final moments.

Yossel's mother was out there looking for her son. After having sent him from Zbaszyn to Otwock, she had changed her mind. With the death of her husband, she was solely responsible for the continuity of her ultra-Orthodox Jewish family. She had two daughters, one with her and one—the rebel in the family—on a Zionist farm in eastern Poland, preparing pioneers for Palestine. Yossel was her only son. What would become of him "out there"? Other mothers heard about her decision and pleaded: "Take my child for yours. Take yours off the train. Put mine on!" As the train left the station, Yossel never knew how close he had come to staying behind; only the pleas from other mothers had made Yossel's mother change her mind again.[7]

Like the rest of us from Otwock, he was looking for a seat. With soldiers standing or sitting in the aisles, the war crowded us together. I remember focusing on the city of Danzig, which had been the subject of so much discussion: Would Germany and Poland fight over it before we got out? What would England do? We were traveling toward Danzig because the port of Gdinya was right next door. After World War I victorious Allies had forced defeated Germany to cede part of its prewar eastern territory to the new Polish state. Danzig, once a thriving German Baltic seaport at the northern end of what had now become a Polish corridor to the sea, was declared a "free city." Almost immediately, postwar Polish governments transformed the village of Gdinya into a major Polish port independent of Germany or the newly established League of Nations. By threatening to end all of these arrangements, Germany was bringing war to our last train stop.

At around five in the morning the train steamed into Danzig and brought a lot of us to the windows of the passageway. I saw concentrations of German soldiers and some tanks. We were so close that I could see one soldier looking through binoculars. What was all the fuss about, I wondered. Germans and their Nazi flags seemed to be everywhere. Until we were actually passing through the Danzig railway station, I had not seen any signs in Polish; as far as I was concerned, the Poles did not have much of a stake in Danzig. I was also relieved that war had not yet broken out here.

Later I wrote to Pappi: "It was morning as we rode past Danzig. This was the town on which everything depended. Then we were in Gdinya. We went into a restaurant where we had breakfast. Then we walked onto the ship [the *Warszawa*]. Hurray! We made it. Now the sea journey can start. After a while it did. The sea was very quiet. Polish warships protect Gdinya. Never before have I seen such a magnificent picture. Only water and sky, and we swish through the sea."[8] Yet I was also afraid. Somehow I knew that Germany had closed the Kiel canal to Polish shipping. That meant we could not sail through this shortcut to England. We would have to go the long way round, through the Kategat and Skagerrack, the waterways between the Baltic and the North Sea. Those straits were notorious for causing seasickness—and I knew it. Our voyage would also take us close to the shores of Denmark and Sweden. What if those countries started fighting just when we were in their waterways?

However, those encounters were still in the future. The task at hand was to settle down to the ship's routines, especially its mealtimes. In comparison to Otwock, the food was wonderful: for the main meal, big pieces of meat, much black bread, and as many hard-boiled eggs as we wanted, mounds of them, served in bowls or soup plates.[9]

Our first breakfast below deck was memorable. Manfred and I were sitting next to each other at one of the long tables. Opposite us sat Yossel, the boy from the general store in Zbaszyn. In Otwock we had seen him often, of course, but we had not become friends. Now, as we ate, something odd happened. Each of us took an egg. I took a second one. But little Yossel—like Manfred, he was between seven and eight years old—reached for a third egg. I said: "Three eggs? No, no third egg. It's not good for you. Two is the limit." He put the egg back into the bowl. With that act of obedience he had bonded himself to us and we to him. From that moment until we separated many months later, we became inseparable, three brothers on an open sea threatening to make us seasick.

Denmark and Sweden remained at peace when we sailed within sight of Copenhagen and Malmo. The guns on the little islands in the channel observed us with the same majestic silence that sounded from the shores, one I never forgot. (Years later, aboard a ferry running between those two cities, I looked around and tried to orient myself in a new place that hinted at familiarity. "I have been here before," I said out loud while recalling that first peaceful passage.)

I had also been wrong about the straits. In place of predicted raging waves, calm seas prevailed and carried us all the way to England. Upon landing in Southampton, we boarded a train for a quick ride to London, where we were taken to a hotel for dinner and a good night's sleep.

What a dinner! The three of us and a few others marveled at the elegantly prepared table setting: white tablecloth and matching napkins, shining cutlery and sparkling drinking glasses—all illuminated by a crystal chandelier—or so I would like to think. At a table next to us, dining alone, was a beautiful blond-haired, white-skinned English lady. She ate so methodically. After swallowing every second mouthful, she lifted her white napkin and wiped the corners of her mouth with it oh so deliberately. I had never seen anybody eat like that.

The next day we met our respective families, who had made their choices from lists identifying single children and siblings. Our family had picked Manfred, myself, and two sisters, Paula and Freda Frajdenreich. The records had not revealed the bonding with Yossel aboard the *Warszawa*, but when the time came for choosing, the tears flowed from a frightened Manfred and Yossel. They wept for all of us! Our family, which had children of its own, took us three boys, two aged seven and one eleven, and two girls, both about the same ages.

How I wish I could remember the details of this selection, to know what was in the hearts and minds of the family that probably saved our lives, even as they knew their country's policy was abandoning our mothers and fathers and so many others like them. These parents and children were willing to share their home with us for God knows how long—and I can't even recall their names.[10]

5

World War II shortened our stay to a few days. We had arrived on August 29. On September 1 Germany invaded Poland; which prompted England to enter the war. As London sent up its barrage balloons to protect against air raids and blackened the upper half of its automobile headlights, we explored the neighborhoods in which our new family lived. It was near Speaker's Corner in Hyde Park, Westminster, with its shops and movie theaters. We also started to attend a parochial school, the Jewish Free School of London. To a four-year veteran of Hamburg's Talmud Torah Schule, the famous parochial school for boys and their male teachers, this London school had the oddest practices. The woman sitting behind a desk, sipping tea from a cup and saucer that matched the teapot on the tray, turned out to be the classroom teacher!

When England declared war against Germany, our lives changed abruptly again.[1] Now there was no way Mutti could sail from Hamburg to Southampton, even on an American ship.[2] The war also meant that Manfred and I would not remain with our new Jewish London family. The British government evacuated children living in London and in other strategic cities. Children enrolled in our Jewish school were sent to the village of Talaton, in Devon, a few hours west of London.

There we had to adjust to a new challenge. Until then we did not have to worry about kosher food or other ritual requirements. Our parents had sent us on a transport with the understanding that we would end up with Jewish caretakers. Talaton was a Christian village rarely frequented by Jews. Now we would have to protect our Jewishness.

I remember feeling that way the moment all of us, each with our visible cardboard name tags, were taken into Talaton's small town hall. I knew we five stood alone on the crowded, scuffed wooden floor that noisy evening since we hardly spoke any English and had shaved heads. We kept our caps on. I was anxious about the treatment we would receive from these villagers, who all looked alike to me. In Germany and in Poland—for all I knew, all over the world—people like them had become our enemies.

Soon the selection process started. Behind the desk at the front someone began calling out names. For us from Otwock it was the third selection within a few days. As in London, the new "parents" in Talaton also preferred sets of brothers and sisters. Thus, Paula and Freda went to one family, while the two Korman brothers were asked to go to another. But we were three! Spontaneously Manfred and Yossel wailed, and this time I, being the senior child at eleven, joined them: three little scared refugee boys in despair, desperately fighting for influence. Polly and Ruth Gosling, mother and daughter, took all three of us. Within a few minutes we arrived at our Christian home, with an English sheepdog named Jock, a black cat named Wiggins, and geese roundabout: Rose Cottage on the Whimple Road.

Mutti and Pappi soon learned of these events. Each had written to us in Otwock and we, in turn, had written to them. With England at war, we had to use Pappi, interned by the still neutral Dutch, as the go-between to Mutti. They did not write about their heartbreaking frustrations. Instead they urged us to write them as much as we could about living in "the country" during the emergency. Fortunately the English postal system knew that Talaton was near Exeter, in Devon, and the people in tiny Talaton knew where we lived. Poor Mutti did not really know: she thought we lived with a Miss Cottage in Talaton, England.

Ignorance about England was our good fortune. Had I been a few years older, I would have been separated from Manfred and interned as an enemy alien, perhaps in the Kitchener camp or on the Isle of Man, where so many Jewish refugee men were interned during the war. I might also have been sent to Canada or, along with hundreds of others—including some ten thousand Christian youngsters—sent to an Australia eager to expand its white population in the face of a feared Asian horde. Then again, all three of us could easily have been sent to one of those English families who exploited their evacuees, especially their Jewish children.[3]

Receiving mail from Mutti and Pappi and being able to write to them was a godsend. It was scary, her being in Germany and he interned in Holland, but I assumed everything would work out. Yossel, Paula, and Freda were not so lucky because their loved ones were in Poland, which was at war with Germany; consequently they had no word from them. Manfred and I also had our Uncle Sally, who was in England. Mutti's youngest brother had emigrated from Elberfeld in 1939. He was one of Kitchener's internees, although we did not know this at the time. We simply assumed he would be there for us if we needed him. Mutti, shuttling between Elberfeld and Hamburg in Nazi Germany, had his address.

Perhaps because the Jewish New Year began on September 14, 1939, just a few days after we had arrived in Devon, I wrote the first letters to Mutti and Pappi as a young Zionist conscious of the Jewish calendar I had been taught to observe. "Dear Father! For Rosheshone [in Hebrew] I wish for you all the best. May G-d guard you in all your ways. With G-d's help may you remain healthy and in each country and city where you are may you be blessed and have a beautiful life. My deepest wish is that next Rosheshone we shall all see each other in Eretz Yisrael [in Hebrew], and Mamma with G-d's help will overcome this dangerous time." The closing remained formal: "These wishes are from your always-thinking-about-you son Gerd." I also enclosed a homemade greeting card for the year 5699.

Within two weeks, when I had not yet received a reply, I wrote "Dear Father" again, urging him, "dear papa" to reply immediately. Then I reported on the school: "Here boys and girls are together. . . . Manfred's English is getting pretty good. . . . The letters here are quite different." I asked how he had fasted on Yomkippur [in Hebrew] and reported that I had fasted until 3 P.M. and Manfred until noon. I inquired about Mutti and asked about his parents in Poland, and requested a favor. "I am sending the first pages of my book, which contains 29 pages. Perhaps you could translate them into English and write them on your typewriter. A boy here wants to put the book in the newspaper.

Please, 'now,' dear Daddy. Answer at once. Love and kisses, your Gerd."

When I received his first letter, I responded: "Please send me immediately a package, if you can: a pair of soccer boots, a suit, a watch, handkerchiefs, and half shoes [not boots]. Do you have enough to eat? Does the package cost customs duty?" To Mutti I wrote: "Dear Mamma, You can imagine how afraid I was about you. At least now I know where you are and how you are managing. . . . Here I am in 6th grade. Oh, in the Talmud Torah [in Hamburg] it was so wonderful." I inquired about friends and relatives and told her I had received a letter from her brother Sally. Then I returned to our new life: "Manfred now has to work hard on his English. Now I first understand why Papa pushed English so hard. My English comes in handy. Dear Mutti. Please, you too must learn English even if its hard. Try. It will come in handy." Briefly assuming that she could somehow come to England, I wrote: "When you come you'll be amazed by the conduct here. Boys don't bow from the waist and girls don't curtsy. I pray [in Hebrew] every day. We are now in the country because of the war [in Hebrew]." At the end of the letter was the first evidence of Manfred's school accomplishments: he was learning how to write!

Rose Cottage was a different house of sojourn. Within a few months we adjusted to Talaton. We quickly mastered the local geography: after closing the gate in front of the cottage, turn left and "carry on" to the junction where Whimple Road meets the road coming from Otterey St. Mary. Turn left again and walk past the town hall, also on the left, straight into the village. Don't turn left but follow the narrow paved lane down the hill to the school and pass through the gate into the church grounds.

In that village—our village—we lived and played. Clothing was a problem. We had none for the winter that was fast approaching. By late October we were still without warm clothes but understood that neither Mutti nor Pappi could send us anything. In time we got some clothing locally. Our uncle wrote letters and sent packages containing English chocolates. We became bicycle riders and reported on our cycling adventures, including spills and punctures. We were knitting wool scarves for ourselves and for the war effort. In early November we joined a few other boys in a foxhunt, which included "60 horses and 20 dogs, along the roads and fields in a pouring rain." Meanwhile it had become obvious to our parents how quickly we were learning English. For the first time in his life, seven-year-old Manfred was becoming literate. Soon he was writing his own notes. In November he congratulated Mutti on her birthday in German, adding: "Hopefully we will all be together." Later he thanked her for telling him that he must be a big boy. And one day he and I started to write notes and letters in English.

We knew nothing of the heartbreaking choices Mutti and Pappi now faced: the American government wanted more and more money from relatives, who were reluctant to pay. In September 1939 the American uncle appeared to have a cash flow problem: $720 of his dollars allocated for Pappi were tied up as a deposit in case Cuba eventually admitted him. Pappi pleaded with the Joint to assume his support needs in Holland, freeing the $720 for getting his family out of Europe. In November 1939 Mutti, then staying with her parents in Elberfeld, in wartime Nazi Germany, received the welcome news that the American consul in Hamburg had been informed that the uncle had deposited another $400 in my mother's name, and that relatives in Connecticut had come forward as guarantors for her and her children upon arrival in the United States. In January 1940 the uncle in Miami wrote to Pappi in Westerbork, informing him that he had deposited $1,000 in Mutti's name so that the American government would not have to support her during her first years in the United States.[4]

The transfer of dollars allowed Mutti to present a completed visa application to the American consul in Hamburg, including the required public documents: Besides a birth certificate and marriage license, there were police reports from Nazi officials in Wuppertal and Hamburg. They stated that she had no criminal record. On January 31, 1940, in the presence of Erich W. Magnuson, Mutti swore that she was a married female of the Hebrew race whose husband "reside[d] at Camp Westerbork, Holland," and that she was the mother of two children who lived in England. She testified that she had resided in Hamburg from 1927 to 1938; in Zbaszyn on the Polish Border from 1938 to July 26, 1939; and in Wuppertal, Germany, since August 30, 1939. Finally, in February 1940, in wartime Nazi Germany, Mutti received the precious "Quota Immigration Visa No. 19225."

In the spring of 1940 Mutti and Pappi tried desperately to at least see each other before she sailed for America, but even that hope was shattered: their efforts to obtain permission for Mutti to stop in Rotterdam met with one delay after another. Then Pappi, interned in the new Westerbork camp not far from Assen, sent the following postcard to Elberfeld: "Let's not wait any longer. If you do not hear [that you can come to Rotterdam] by the 13th [of April], sail from Genoa. Surely everything is for the best. Don't wait any longer." Within a month German bombs were falling on Rotterdam and parachutists dropped from the sky over the Hague. When, heartbroken, she sailed from Genoa, Mutti sent us the following final message from Europe, written on a picture postcard aboard the U.S. ship *Washington:* "Now Mutti sails all alone. Ach, I am so sad that you are not with me. Hopefully you will follow soon."[5]

When we finally received the wonderful news that she was out of Germany—the card had reached us in Talaton via Brooklyn, New York—Passover had come and gone. That was the holiday when, one year earlier, in 1939, we had all been together for the last time, in Nadnia, where we had celebrated spiritual freedom in a Polish refugee camp. Now Mutti celebrated hers with other passengers, partaking of a kosher seder aboard the *Washington,* while Pappi celebrated his seder in a Dutch refugee camp outside the village of Westerbork, in the middle of nowhere.

Manfred and I were part of the caring household of the Goslings in Devon, where we and Yossel had become part of their family. On Christmas morning three stuffed stockings had greeted us from the fireplace, and each of our pieces of plumb pudding had a threepence hidden inside. Sunday mornings Polly's son, Tom, let us assist him in ringing the village church bells. On the first night of Passover I was encouraged to conduct a seder for Manfred and Yossel, as well as for Paula and Freda.

By the gracious leave of the Anglican mistress of Rose Cottage, the three of us had established a Jewish presence. We refused to eat meat and the Goslings respected our wishes. In the correspondence between Mutti and myself, it took a long time before either of us acknowledged the female members of the Gosling household in any other way except "the lady" or "the ladies." That was the reason why Mutti had addressed the postcard from

Author, Manfred, and Yossel in Talaton, England, 1940.

the *Washington* care of "Cottage" and had sent greetings to Miss Cottage.

Perhaps Ruth Gosling understood how Mutti and I, who each felt the presence of a possible new catastrophe, were unable to acknowledge that another family had become dear to us. I had not written that she had renamed me Gerhardt in order to protect me from ridicule: in the English press there was a character named Gerti Gestapo! She had also renamed Yossel "Joseph" and had begun to call him "Joe"; Manfred's name did not have to be Anglicized and thus remained "unconverted." The occasional corrections in a firm hand in black ink, especially Manfred's halting efforts in writing in English, make it obvious that Miss Gosling read and helped us with our letters. Around Passover she wrote a special note in broken German to celebrate Mutti's arrival in the United States. Later I began to send regards from Ruth and Mother Gosling.[6]

London's organized Jewry helped with our seder preparations in Talaton, but when I asked permission it was the Goslings who made it possible. As part of the evacuated day school, we belonged to a larger group connected to Jewish officials. Our one-room schoolhouse—where six grades were taught, one per row—was run by one-armed Mr. Cohn, the teacher who had contact with Jews in London and in Exeter. Our matzo supply was part of a larger Passover package that included salami, cakes, candies, chocolates, marmalade, and tea. I don't remember what the children from London did on Passover. Perhaps they went home or their parents came to visit in mid-April, when the "phony war" on the Continent still becalmed English society. For one Passover lunch we three Gosling boys went to Exeter for a splendid family meal. Each of us also received a raincoat; for the spring rains had come to Devon.

The seder was memorable. The five of us sat at a prepared table, with a white tablecloth and matching napkins, plates plus cutlery, and sparkling drinking glasses. "This year I took Pappi's place," I wrote Mutti, "specifically at the seder [in Hebrew]." We had "no bitter herbs [in Hebrew] and no charoset [in Hebrew]. Moreover," because mother and daughter Gosling would not allow children to drink spirits, "we had only matzos [in Hebrew] and instead of wine we had water." The seder "lasted only one hour," not long at all compared to the time we were accustomed to sit at our family seder table. I closed the letter with an amended passage from the Haggadah. Toward the end of every seder participants then usually exclaimed or sang "Next Year in Jerusalem." I wrote the passage in Hebrew, adding "U.S.A." in parentheses.[7]

Part III

Miller Avenue of East New York

6

Soon thereafter America beckoned. One day a uniformed Uncle Sally appeared at school. After a few days' leave following his participation in the famed English troop evacuation from French channel ports, he had taken the train from London, found his way to Rose Cottage, and was sent by Miss Gosling to the school. To Gerhardt and Manfred she assigned Jock, with whom we slept, played, and came to school regularly, and Jock had brought our soldier uncle into the classroom.

He looked just as I had remembered him from our last visit to Elberfeld, a little taller than Mutti, his older sister. Teacher Cohn excused us and we, together with Jock, walked back to the cottage to hear about Uncle Sally's adventures among the French allies, whom he did not like, and his encounter with "terrible" English barbers, who were rank amateurs when it came to cutting his thick, wavy hair. We also learned how active he had been in trying to arrange for our departure to the United States. I was even concerned that he was spending "all of his money on us."[1]

Now it was our turn to get the runarounds especially reserved for stateless refugees. In early May we cycled to nearby Sidmouth Junction, parked our bicycles, and caught the train to Paddington for a week's stay in London. At the station the "Committee" person we had counted on to meet us was not there. So amidst all too familiar sounds of railway stations, we waited endlessly on a wooden bench on an empty platform. We had nowhere to go and no one to call. At long last a woman headed straight for us, checked our name tags, mumbled something about being late, and asked: "What's that sticking out of your

Uncle Sally in the uniform of a British soldier, 1940.

raincoat pocket?" I replied: "An account of our wanderings." She asked if she could read it, promising "I'll have it back to you in the morning." I never saw it again.

The business at hand involved clerks, visas, and boat tickets. I wrote Mutti from the Newstead residence at "No. 2 Gulyon Avenue, Hernhill, London S.E. 24": "Dear Mummi!," I began in German,

I am now in London with Manfred for the visa. On Wednesday we were at the Consulate. I wrote everything on a paper. I believe you know how they do these things. The problem was that we had no passport and no birth certificates. So we had to apply for a document that made us legally stateless. But the Committee will arrange all that. According to them, you bought a ship ticket. But you bought the ship ticket at the wrong company. So they had to take it out and buy the ticket from another company. (I have not got the visa yet [I added the English translation in parentheses and then repeated the phrase in German], but we will get it.) When I know the sailing date of the ship, I will write you immediately, then you can pick us up at the port. That would be glorious.

There were forebodings. "Manfred is all right. Just now he is looking out of the window and looks at the [London] people and autos going by, just the same as in Hamburg." I reminded Mutti, who was then in New York, of the time when Manfred would sit for hours observing life on the street below. I asked: "Do you hear anything from Pappi? Yesterday I talked with a gentleman from Holland and he told me that where Pappi lives there were no fights and no air raids. So don't worry." I added the following P.S.: "We have saved 4 dollars. That's a lot for us."[2]

During the following weeks in Devon we pretended that nothing had changed but it was no use. Uncle Sally's visit and our trip to the consulate changed everything. Right after my birthday in July, eight-year-old Manfred caught the glum mood. He wrote the following letter to "Dear Mummie!" in English: "We Have Spent a very Happy Day for Gerd's Birthday. Presents, and a Cake With 12 Candles on it. We Were Very Pleased To See Uncle Sally. He Did Look Nice As a Soldier. We Are Going to Have 5 Weeks Holiday From School, And We Are Going To Do War Works. I wonder when our boat will sail. I hope it will be soon. Much regards and love from your Manfred xxxxxxxxxxxxx"

It was hard to think of leaving. When we mounted our waiting bicycles at Sidmouth Junction and rode back to Rose Cottage, we felt homeward bound. It was bad enough to say good-bye to the Goslings and the village of Talaton. At the time I knew only that I had come to care deeply for its people, its roads and fields and hedges, its morning fogs, its honking geese and barking dogs. Today I realize that the tiny Christian shelter had saved what was left of our childhood when we had arrived the year before. The Goslings had cared for three quite consciously Jewish boys: once a week they had bathed us in a freestanding tub filled with hot water from the kettle. Then they dried us. Mother Gosling had cut our toenails.

They and their neighbors had made me feel important. I was given various responsibilities: plant and harvest a little victory garden; clean a chicken coop (with the aid of the gas mask I always carried in my container); and run errands on foot or with the aid of the bicycle I had come to call my own. The Goslings trusted us. We cycled into nearby Ottery St. Mary and once even to Sidmouth on the Channel coast. To this day I treasure the memory of Jock and Wiggins sharing the spoils of the cat's morning rabbit hunt and eating from the same plate; Wiggins quietly waited while the bigger Jock took care to leave her portion. In the Goslings' Talaton everyone seemed to care for one another.

To say good-bye to Yossel was heartbreaking and remains so to this day. He really had become a brother in every way. We had shared so much, including the big upstairs bed in which we slept and wetted night after night! The three of us had become a presence in Rose Cottage and in the village. Paula and Hedwig lived close by, but in that first year we never bonded with them the way the three of us bonded with each other. Once around Christmastime we even performed together in the town hall before the entire village, singing songs we had learned since coming to Talaton. To the tune of "Danny Boy" I soloed with "In Derry Vale," and as a trio we offered our rendition of "Little Brown Jug."

As our departure approached, I talked with Miss Gosling about Yossel. I asked her what would happen to him after we left. She said that she and her mother would await any news from his mother. If there were none, they would adopt him as their son. I assumed everything would work out for the best. In

CERTIFICATE OF IDENTITY.
CERTIFICAT D'IDENTITE.

Valid until 14th January, 1941.
Valable jusqu'

The present certificate is issued for the sole purpose of providing the holder with identity papers in lieu of a national passport. It is without prejudice to and in no way affects the national status of the holder. If the holder obtains a national passport it ceases to be valid and must be surrendered to the issuing authority.

Le présent certificat est délivré à seule fin de fournir au titulaire une pièce d'identité pouvant tenir lieu de passeport national. Il ne préjuge pas la nationalité du titulaire et est sans effet sur celle-ci. Au cas où le titulaire obtiendrait un passeport national, ce certificat cessera d'être valable et devra être renvoyé à l'autorité qui l'a délivré.

Signature of Holder,
Signature du titulaire.

Gerd Kormann

DESCRIPTION.
SIGNALEMENT.

Age / Age .... 11.

Height / Taille .... 4 ft. 8 in.

Hair / Cheveux .... Brown.

Eyes / Yeux .... Brown.

Face / Visage .... Oval.

Nose / Nez .... Small.

Special peculiarities / Signes particuliers ....

Remarks / Observations

This Certificate is available during its validity for the holder's return to the United Kingdom without visa.

Durant la période de sa validité le présent certificat sera valable pour la rentrée du titulaire dans le Royaume Uni sans formalité de visa.

This Certificate must be endorsed with an Exit Permit for Embarkation and Visaed by a British Consular Authority abroad for return to the United Kingdom.

Surname / Nom de famille. .... KORMANN.

Forenames / Prénoms. .... Adolf, Gerd.

Date of birth / Date de naissance. .... 24th July, 1928.

Place of birth / Lieu de naissance. .... Elberfeld.

Nationality of origin / Nationalité d'origine. .... German.

Surname and forenames of Father / Nom de famille et prénoms du père. .... KORMANN Osias.

Surname and forenames of Mother / Nom de famille et prénoms de la mère. .... LAUFER Rosa.

Name of wife (husband) / Nom de la femme (mari). ....

Names of children / Noms des enfants. ....

Occupation / Profession. ....

Former residence abroad / Ancien domicile à l'étranger. .... Hamburg.

Present residence in the United Kingdom / Résidence actuelle dans le Royaume Uni. .... 2, Gubyon Avenue,

Herne Hill, London, S.E.24.

Police Registration Certificate / Certificat d'enregistrement délivré par la Police. ....

The undersigned certifies that the photograph and signature hereon are those of the holder of the present document.

Le soussigné certifie que la photographie et la signature apposées ci-contre sont bien celles du porteur du présent document.

Signature of the issuing authority,
Signature de l'autorité.

JBkuznov

H.M. CHIEF INSPECTOR,
IMMIGRATION BRANCH,
HOME OFFICE,
LONDON, S.W.1.

CERTIFICATE OF IDENTITY FEE.	7/6 1816

Author's Certificate of Identity, July 15, 1940.

any event, I knew there was nothing I could do. We could not take him with us to America—English and American officials had seen to that.

In the last days of August 1940, on the eve of the Luftwaffe's major campaign against London's civilians, Manfred and I returned to London with three bound-up cartons of clothing in tow. After experiencing one or two ear-piercing air raid alarms and hiding in a shelter refuge in a blacked-out railway station, we met our chaperones for the trip north. These strangers, a couple assigned by the Joint, were now in charge of our transportation. Together we stole through the night to Glasgow, the Atlantic port on Scotland's west coast. The morning of August 31 we boarded the *Cameronia*, a single-stack passenger ship belonging to the Anchor Line, which was about to start its solo run through German submarine–infested waters of the Atlantic.

Everything about this ship and our voyage was different from our experience aboard the *Warszawa*. We were no longer part of an organized group of scared children ashamed of their shaved heads, plus we understood the language of the crew! Confident and optimistic, Manfred and I were just two children going home to our Mutti in America. Except at mealtimes, we rarely saw our chaperones. We had free run of the *Cameronia*. The voyage was an adventure filled with fun and games.

During the first few days it was exciting to see a solitary friendly aircraft flying overhead. But then it was gone. "Now we're too far out, too far from land, for RAF protection," a friendly sailor said; he did not explain to us that we had passed the line on the map where British air or naval escort for merchant ships ended. Nor did he tell us—or perhaps he did not know either—of the many English ships the German U-boats were then sinking along the course of our run.[3] Not until we reached New York harbor, seven days later, did we learn about the submarine that had followed us much of the way.

Our major problem was seasickness. It struck on the first day in the open sea. "On one day I was seasick 5 times. Manfred 6 times," I reported to Pappi in Holland. "We went down to the dining room but had to run upstairs again to the deck, else we would have puked while eating. At the noon meal the same thing happened. We ran upstairs again. As I passed the lifeboats I began to puke, I tell you, like I have never puked before. All this time Manfred is standing next to me, laughing, naturally. But when I finished I felt like a new person." After that we did not puke again, even though "the next day the sea was much rougher. The waves were fairly high so that one washed over the railing."[4]

We walked in and out of the accommodations set aside for second- and first-class passengers. Manfred and I slept and ate in the third-class section, where I vaguely remember the service was fine. But soon we wanted more. One day we decided to visit another class. First we tried the sinks and toilets. Then we took a bath in "their" tub. It was great fun, even when we scooted out in response to angry voices on the other side of the door, which we had locked.

At 6:05 P.M. on September 9 we passed Sandy Hook and soon joined other passengers looking at the shore. Without a blackout or barrage balloons, New York City's lights twinkled their greetings. We were coming home. Tomorrow would be the big day when government inspectors would come on board to check our papers and verify our health. Once they cleared us, we would be free to walk down the gangplank to embrace Mutti. She would be waiting. To be certain, I or someone on my behalf sent a telegram: ARRIVE WITH ANCHOR LINE ON TUESDAY.[5] Before we went to sleep, the *Cameronia* had come to a halt, just like the *St. Louis* in Havana that Pappi had written about. But this was different. I was confident. Manfred and I would be allowed to leave, just like Mutti on the *Washington,* our pioneer on American soil.

Shortly after breakfast we all climbed out on deck and were stunned by the harbor view. There to the left we saw her, the Statue of Liberty. Slowly the *Cameronia,* assisted by a tugboat, entered New York City, past endless piers until we finally reached the moorings. Now it was our turn to tie the last knots of our cartons as well as gain release from official clerical entanglements. Then we would be free to find Mutti.

Beside herself with worry about the wartime hazards of the ocean, on this fateful Tuesday morning a relative had brought her to the port early. At Pier 95 she told everyone within earshot about the arrival of her two little boys. As the crowd grew, so did anticipation, especially when the *Cameronia* began to discharge its passengers. Mutti had acquired a veritable support group of strangers all looking intensely at the gangplank.[6]

Our discharge procedure in one of the ship's lounges was perfunctory. All the papers were in order and we answered all the questions properly, using the King's English with a Talaton dialect; since the fall of 1939—except perhaps to the keenest of ears or when we were exhausted—we had lost our German accents. We collected our boxes, joined the line, and found ourselves walking down the gangplank. As soon as I saw Mutti looking up at us, calling me by my nickname ("Bubi"), I blanked out the cheering crowd. I started to sing "Lustig ist das Zigeuner Leben tra la la la" (Merry is the Gypsy's life) a sort of farewell anthem to our homeless past, over and over again until we were in Mutti's arms.

She led us into the dimly lit, noisy subway system. Along the way we each asked and answered countless questions about all the yesterdays of our separation. Between hugs and kisses, fragments of thoughts crossed our lips in German. In addition, we were anxious about the station where we had to get out. Suddenly I realized that even in America the worst might happen: Mutti had no place of her own. More separation. More wandering! Where to now? Her address provided the clue, which, given my ignorance of New York's Jewish demography, I could not appreciate: c/o Levin, 4 Stonehenge Road, Great Neck, N.Y. Mutti worked there as a live-in housekeeper, had done so since the National Council of Jewish Women (NCJW) had helped her to find this, her first job in America. Having arrived without any means of support, she now had to live on what she earned, and that was not enough to set up an apartment of her own in Great Neck, an exclusive suburb on the North Shore of Long Island. Instead, she had found the Petrovers, acquaintances from Hamburg, who said we could stay with them if Mutti would pay for our room and board. It all tumbled out as her sad eyes lovingly tried to hide the pain of American life.

When she had arrived in April, an official from the NCJW had met the boat and took her to a family named Oelbaum, one of the relatives whose name and address she had written in her notebook. "He would not leave the front door of my relatives until they had promised to take me in for the night." Next she had gone to other relatives who lived in East New York, Brooklyn, and to those on Pappi's side, who lived on the Lower East Side. Everywhere she sought support affidavits to bring Pappi from Holland, or guarantor money to satisfy government officials in

Cuba and in Amsterdam. Her own income was meager, certainly not enough to support us and to pay the weekly bus and subway fares on the one day she had off to visit us in Brooklyn.

There was another reason we could not live in Great Neck: it was not Jewish enough. Our parents had also been concerned about Christian Rose Cottage. Some weeks after arriving at our new Brooklyn address in East New York, I wrote Pappi in German, "We go to synagogue every Shabbes. We also attend a Jewish school every day. So you need not worry at all. Besides, for almost the entire year we ate no meat and did not forget our Jewishness."[7] Mutti would not even consider rearing us in the neighborhood where she lived because there we could not grow up as the modern traditional Jews she wanted us to become, no matter how hard she tried. Thus, it had to be a room in a stranger's apartment.

The Canal Street subway station caught us by surprise. As she cried out, "Raus, raus, wir changing hier," she reached for a carton with one hand and for Manfred with the other. I grabbed the strings of each of the other boxes and dragged them through the door of the subway car. On the platform I let go. One box broke. Shirts and underwear scattered around our shoes. That was too much. I cried uncontrollably, perhaps the first such tears and sobs since we had left Mutti in Zbaszyn.

7

That night at the Petrovers, the kind and generous Oelbaums arrived, bearing fall clothing for their unfortunate refugee relatives. Our Rose Cottage confidence tempered our anxiousness among these new strangers. I knew what it was like to be among strangers without knowing their language. Now I could trust my recently acquired Talaton English in this new world. Manfred and I were first embarrassed and then excited to receive what the Oelbaums called new knickers. To this day I have often wondered if Mutti understood the ensuing exchange:

"Knickers is what girls wear."

"Not here, not in America. Come try them on. They are boys pants, made out of corduroy, with elastic at the bottom of each leg."

"Oh. They are knickerbockers!"

Everything fit, more or less. Mutti beamed through tears of gratefulness. She felt our excitement. We had received the first new clothing since Hamburg. The Oelbaums and the Petrovers immediately turned to the question of the hour: "How do you like America?" Having just arrived and having been so disappointed in not being able to go home, we did not know what to say to them and to all the others who in the next weeks and months repeatedly asked us the same question.

We were beginning six American years of sojourning in different lodgings, Mutti in Great Neck and Manfred and myself in East New York. We were physically living apart, and yet we acted as a family convinced that Pappi would return from Holland and then we would be together again in our own apartment, just like before. Part of us remained unchanged even as we

84

felt ourselves becoming different persons, more and more like New York people.

Mutti managed our lives from afar, occasionally when I phoned her from a public telephone, but most decidedly on her weekly visits, some of which she turned into visits to relatives as well as educational and cultural events. With the help of the Jewish Child Care Association (JCCA) she found us homes with Jews who kept kosher and lived in Jewish neighborhoods, hoping that both would do right by us.

Mutti introduced us to her favorite relatives, the Kormans, who lived in Manhattan on Lewis Street, near Delancey Street and the Williamsburg Bridge. One of the sons, Meyer, became our hero, even before he joined the air force and completed twenty-five missions as a group bombardier over Germany. He introduced us to his neighborhood, which was quite different from ours in East New York—his had drunks who hung out in alleys and hallways, plus violent youth gangs—and arranged for us to become no-fee campers at the Grand Street Settlement House's Camp Moodna in Mountainville, New York. There we made friends with black boys who spoke a smattering of Yiddish. On one of our visits, when Manfred and I were still learning how to navigate New York by ourselves, we boarded the BMT subway line at the Van Sicklen Avenue station without realizing that we had no change for the trip home. Near the Williamsburg Bridge plaza we learned that New York policemen could be trusted to come through: one of them gave me two nickels, which was enough subway fare to get home.

Mutti put us in touch with Jewish organizations and events outside the neighborhoods in which we lived. She told us about war news reported in the popular newspaper *Aufbau*, which was published by the New World Club, a social and athletic organization of German-speaking Jews in New York. She fretted about our public education, often supplementing it by visiting the local library and bringing home books she thought I should read in German, like Erich Maria Remarque's classic World War I novel: *Im Westen Nichts Neues (All Quiet on the Western Front)* and *Der Weg Zurück (The Road Back)*. Occasionally we attended free lectures and Schubert lieder recitals; once in a while we even attended performances of Verdi, Puccini, and Bizet operas (Mutti's favorite composers) at the Metropolitan Opera. How she found

Manfred and author at Camp Moodna, a Grand Street Settlement House camp located in Mountainville, New York, ca. 1941.

the money to pay for the tickets I'll never know, for even the ones way up in the balcony were expensive for her. (Up here, she reminded us, real experts come to listen, to hear how well the voices carry!) Not once did she ever suggest that we quit school as soon as possible in order to earn some money. The thought would never have occurred to her—or to us.

Pappi participated in our lives with an occasional "Red Cross" letter from Westerbork. Some weeks before my Bar Mitzvah, in the summer of 1941—before the United States had entered the war but a year after the Germans had conquered Holland—I received a special letter. We did not know that while Westerbork was still being administered by Dutch authorities, he had played a leading role organizing Jewish religious and cultural activities for hundreds of people in the camp. He had stepped forward for the same reason he had done so in Nadnia: regardless of the circumstances, Jews had to have a religious and cultural center. He had started his organizing activities in November 1939, when the camp was still small. "You gave it your all," a fellow inmate and synagogue official wrote him in March 1941 when their so-called congregation numbered almost a thousand. "In no small measure we owe you our synagogue, its daily minyan, and its regular services on Shabbes and on the High Holy Days."[1]

His Bar Mitzvah letter, written a few months later, said nothing about his imprisonment in a camp organized and administered for the Germans by the Dutch. In fact, he all but pretended that I was still the same child from Hamburg, about to enter my teens: "This change is celebrated; it is one of the most beautiful celebrations which a person in his lifetime experiences. It is an experience that buries itself deeply in a person's innermost being. And it is one in which parents yearn to participate. I cannot be there; my dream has not come to pass; the Heavens wanted it otherwise. I do not want to complain. I thank the Creator that your mother and brother are with you and that I can be with you in my thoughts." From afar in Westerbork he reminded me: "To grow up properly one needs to call on reason for assistance, to determine rationally right from wrong. In the battle between reason and emotion one has to remember one's obligation. Learn early to become master of your feelings, hold yourself in control, practice self-discipline." He closed by reminding me of Judaism's claim on me, a Bar Mitzvah: "Your responsibility to

Judaism is weighty. It demands sacrifice throughout one's life. Reach for it, shoulder it, even though it makes life hard and the struggle toward the Light difficult. Judaism's roots penetrate so deeply into the earthly kingdom that they sustain us in the worst of storms to which we are exposed."[2]

I am not certain how much of an impact that letter made. I have read it often and felt its strength. But that was a different time. War was ever-present, in mind and emotions, for all around us relatives and friends lived in another world, one of peace; they did not, as we did, fear the next possible catastrophe or that instant of panic every time a police or ambulance siren sounded an air raid for us. Yet I also lived in their world. When I replied, I thanked Pappi in one brief sentence for his beautiful letter and turned immediately to my concerns. I am getting "Barmitzvo" lessons "without cost because, of course, I am a refugee. In school things are pretty good. Grades are different here than in Germany. The best grade is 100% and the worst is 0%. I am also learning with %. Now I understand how the companies [in Germany] dealt with you. . . . . How are you? Can you still come to my Barmitzvo? . . . Hebrew school is very easy here. I also receive it for free."

By now Manfred and I were living with the Rifkin family in our third shelter, located at 392 Miller Avenue, in a neighborhood where lower-middle-class and middle-class Jews bumped into each other in the stores, but where they slept in very different apartments and houses. After a few months with the Petrovers, we had been asked to leave. As a temporary arrangement, we moved in with the mother-in-law of an Engelberg living at 65 Richmond Street. She lived in modest quarters of a large house, which she shared with her son, who had married a granddaughter of Mutti's uncle in Miami, and his wife's parents. In my mind the house reflected the wealth and luxury I had come to associate with rich Uncle Engelberg. When he came north to visit, he stayed with these children of his.

We handled moving in with the Rifkins in stride because we did not change the fundamental fixtures of our lives: Mutti, and P.S. 76, the public school we began to attend the week after we tried on our first pair of knickers. After duly reporting our address changes to Miss Eleanor J. Spitznagle, our severe-looking

principal, and to our kind and generous 6B and 2A grade teachers, we walked the seventeen blocks from Richmond Street, our
sandwiches and books in tow; later this was reduced to the seven
blocks from Miller Avenue—without sandwiches, however, for
kind parents of school chums who lived closer invited us to join
them for a kosher lunch. At P.S. 76 everyone came to know and
respect us, not as the school's refugees or its only "green" immigrants but as P.S. 76 pupils who had come to America as Jewish
refugees. In seventh grade I became chief of the aides; for graduation from 8B on January 27, 1943, the class had chosen me salu-
tatorian. The entries in my "Autographs P.S. 76" book barely
hinted at a European past: Among "My Favorites" I listed *Berlin
Diary* for "Book," "Shira" for "Author," and "soccer" for "Sport."
One page read "Reserved for My Dad," but it was blank. The
other pages recorded cliched expressions appropriate at graduation time, including the sentiments Manfred and Mutti recorded
in my book.

That feeling of acceptance probably explains why I refused to
leave P.S. 76. The rabbi of the Orthodox synagogue at the corner
of Glenmore and Miller Avenues, where we attended afternoon
school, found a way to subsidize my tuition at a day school
called "Haim Berlin." Somehow he persuaded Mutti, and reluctantly I tried it. It was a disaster. I compared it not only to P.S. 76
but also to the Talmud Torah I had attended in Hamburg: Discipline was poor and the teachers were pedagogical nitwits.
Besides, I also thought the schedule was barbaric, from eight until
four in the afternoon. The rabbi, my teachers, and Mutti somehow
did not realize how much P.S. 76 had come to mean to me. At the
end of the week, I quit and went back to P.S. 76.

On Miller Avenue Manfred and I grew up in different circles.
A nine-year-old, his friends were the children of neighbors who
lived in the same apartment house. He also formed friendships
through buddies and their parents, like Dr. David Anderman and
his family, who lived in private homes down the street, toward
Sutter Avenue, where the middle classes owned homes, rather
than across the street, northward toward Pitkin Avenue, where
the lower middle classes lived in tenement dwellings. Except for
our walks to P.S. 76 and excursions with Mutti on her days off
from work, there were few reasons for Manfred to leave the
neighborhood. Even after graduating from P.S. 76, he remained

near home by attending Thomas Jefferson High School, located eight blocks to the southwest. He and the neighborhood were inseparable: that's where he played and hung out, where he found his part-time jobs. I did, too, but being the oldest Mutti trusted me to venture beyond Miller Avenue, first with an upstairs neighbor. When he asked if I wanted to come to work with him on Sunday morning, I took the subway with him. He brought me to his loft on West Twenty-eighth Street, where he showed me how to help him unroll layer after layer of clothing material on a long cutting table. In the afternoon we were back on Miller Avenue.

By 1943 I was riding subways all over the city, starting and returning from the different stations along Van Sicklen Avenue; for by then I was a student at Brooklyn Technical High School and a member of the athletic division of the New World Club. The school was at the western end of Brooklyn, a thirty-minute ride on the old Pitkin elevated train line. Because of its waist-high metal mechanical doors attached to open-air platforms at the end of each car, a conductor had to move two levers for each door to open them. Each weekday a few of us from Brooklyn Tech took that train from the Van Sicklen station; however, in my junior year I did not return home that way. During the school year, Artie Levine, a dear friend from P.S. 76, found part-time jobs for us with the *New York Journal-American* as delivery boys assigned to a supervisor in charge of the Times Square area in Manhattan.[3] At the end of the school day, we caught the BMT subway at Dekalb Avenue and made our way to the old Metropolitan Opera House building, toward the front of the side entrance with the coffee shop. There, while waiting for our newspaper editions, we played chess and talked to friends or wives of famous singers; once we schmoozed long enough with a woman and her poodle to meet her husband, the tenor Gerhard Pechner. About five times in the afternoon and early evening truckers dumped bales consisting of a hundred newspapers on the sidewalk. The supervisor sorted them and gave each of us our bundle. We lifted them on our shoulders, carried them through dense and noisy early-evening midtown traffic, and delivered them to newsstands in our zone. By 6:30 P.M. we headed back to Van Sicklen Avenue.

Since Brooklyn Tech carefully selected its student body from all over New York City, my school chums in high school were most always different from neighborhood buddies, especially once the

Author, Mutti, and Manfred, 1943-44.

school had its own soccer team, its first since the 1920s. Having played European-style football on the streets and fields of Hamburg, Otwock, and Talaton, I was Brooklyn Tech's most experienced soccer player! Instantly I acquired a new social status—at least among my classmates, who always gave me a loud send-off when, as captain of the squad, I could leave my English class early to join my teammates for the game that afternoon.

The New World Club drew me into a network outside of East New York.[4] During my first year in high school I joined the club's junior soccer squad, which played scheduled matches on Sundays in New York's Eastern District Soccer League. This was serious business. Under Walter Stoerger and then Max Berger, our devoted coaches, I was playing in my immigrant peer group, some seasons as captain of a squad usually consisting of German- and English-speaking teenagers. In order to arrive punctually for the ten o'clock warm-up whistle, from late summer into spring every Sunday morning, I was on the BMT, IND, or IRT subway line, riding forty-five minutes or more to Sterling Oval, our home pitch in the Bronx, to Astoria in Queens, or an hour and a half if the game was held in Van Cortland Park. Many on my team became friends, reflecting an alternative-youth culture vastly different from that of East New York.

The culture of discipline governing the games contained complex New York City ethnic tensions that were rife in our league.[5] Every now and then—especially when we played the "German Hungarians"—group violence threatened. I had seen it erupt on only two other occasions, each quite different from those ignited by a soccer match. The first occurred on Miller Avenue when a gang consisting of about ten teenagers came into our neighborhood and began to tear up the Yiddish-language newspapers displayed outside "Mr. Fleischer's" candy store at the corner of Miller and Belmont Avenues. "Our big guys" immediately confronted them and both sides almost came to blows. The second time was far worse and involved Jews beating up Jews during halftime of a basketball game held on the court of the Grand Street Settlement House. Out of nowhere a mob of teenagers came tearing into the gym, chasing one lonely fugitive. They caught him, pinned him to a chair, beat him to a pulp, and dragged him outside—all this witnessed by passive spectators.

Author's New World Club soccer team, 1945–46.

At the beginning of the second half, in a tied game with the German Hungarians, their forwards signaled to each other and to us that the match would turn nasty, which it did, but without getting out of control. However, after the game, as we were heading to the subway, we saw "them" waiting for us at the streetcorner. I knew the confrontation would turn ugly when, as captain of our squad, I began walking toward their captain and noticed my neighborhood friend and teammate Ludwig Schorr hanging back with a big rock in his hand. Each captain knew the Jewish refugees in America would give as good as they got from the children whose parents we associated with New York City's Nazi-oriented German-American Bund in the late 1930s and early 1940s. Fortunately they let us go home without a street brawl.

The New World Club network stretched beyond my teammates to older players, their fathers, and to the league's official doctor, Morris Dessauer. Herbie, an older player, and his marvelous little Pappa Schainholz would watch our team play. In 1944, before Herbie was drafted, they both befriended Manfred and me; I often took Manfred to the games, and in time he joined as a player himself. Sometimes the Schainholzes would bring us to their apartment on Morningside Heights, near Riverside Church. On one of my first visits Herbie said: "You know who visits our painter friend in the apartment above us? Einstein!"

In retrospect, Dr. Dessauer was a father figure. A passionate soccer enthusiast, he was the league's official doctor and, as such, administered to any player on a team sponsored by the New World Club. I had to see him because I developed a "deranged meniscus" in my right knee. Often it "jumped" and locked, causing intense pain for a few days. Regular diathermic treatment was one way to aid recovery; Dr. Dessauer, whose office was located on Fifty-eighth Street, between Sixth and Seventh Avenues, had the right machine. Once a week for many weeks I would schlep up to his office, discovering new worlds as I passed Carnegie Hall and other famous landmarks. Somehow, this jovial, balding, chubby man always found time to talk to me about my general well being. I knew I was a good player, a fast, competitive soccer-savvy halfback or forward—even a star among the junior players of the city. But the friendship of the club doctor went beyond his passion for soccer. I trusted him and sought his advice on many subjects.

Except perhaps for Manny's Dr. Anderman, who was our "free" physician—he never charged us anything, not even when he arranged for my free knee surgery—we had no one like Dr. Dessauer in our Miller Avenue neighborhood, certainly not the Rifkins. They fed and sheltered us properly, responsibly, and even caringly. But their values were different from ours. Manfred and I again became a distinctive presence, this time in a kosher household. Each of us invented symbols to remind us that we were sojourners far from the home we longed for. I would not open the refrigerator door without permission.

The Rifkins, a couple in their midfifties, were janitors, living rent-free in an apartment house owned by the "Brandel" branch of the Engelbergs. Brandel and her children lived a few blocks south of us in one of those middle-class houses of the larger neighborhood. We were the poor, needy refugee relatives who had to be helped. When Mutti went looking for new lodgings while we were squatting on Richmond Street, Brandel approached the Rifkins because she knew their three grown children were beginning to leave the apartment and therefore the Rifkins could use the extra money.

Mr. Rifkin, a small, hunched over, sickly looking man with a saturnine countenance, occasionally worked as a blacksmith. In the building we helped him to shovel coal into the boiler and to collect garbage by hauling a dumbwaiter. It was manually operated, running along ropes behind kitchen apartments. Tenants would simply pull up the empty dumbwaiter, open the doors, stack or sometimes dump the refuse into the enclosed frame, close the doors, and go about their business. In time the dumbwaiter filled up, and if it was not emptied often enough, the garbage spilled all over the shaft, preventing the doors from closing and causing it to get stuck! Sometimes we cleaned it out. Then, for fun, we crawled into the dumbwaiter and pulled ourselves up and down behind the neighbors' kitchens. From our secret hiding place we could overhear their conversations.

Missus—that's what we called Mrs. Rifkin—was a stout, energetic, sweaty woman who set the tone with her good intentions and shrill voice. We heard it often, in foul-mouthed arguments with her daughter and, whenever they were home, with her two older sons. I had never before heard such language, but now this gutter talk and imagery was becoming part of our vocabulary and imagination. Missus was indifferent to much of our conduct, but Manfred and I did have to cope with her brusque directives. She was in an awkward position. Her sons—and her daughter in particular—also tried to tell us what to do. And there was Mutti. Even though we considered Mutti our highest authority, for Missus young absentee Mutti was a German-accented refugee greenhorn who did not know how to raise stuttering, bed-wetting Jewish youngsters. Missus sent us into the street to hang out with the other children. "Go play! Go out and play," she commanded when we came home from school or in the evening, after dinner, or even on a Friday night. On Shabbes, when we came home from the synagogue and had our lunch, she gave us money to go to the movie house around the corner on Sutter Avenue.

Miller Avenue Movie Theater, East New York, Brooklyn, 1945.

Manfred and I had fun on the "street." On Friday nights we cruised Sutter Avenue on foot. At the movies we saw all the episodes of "Captain Marvel" or "The Green Hornet." We started to speak the fractured neighborhood Yiddish. I even forged Mrs. Rifkin's signature in Yiddish when I needed a note for the scary dean of students at Brooklyn Tech to explain my absence. However, I knew all was not right in a world where friends swiped candy bars and their older siblings found sex on top of wooden milk crates belonging to the local grocery store.

I was old enough to have serious homework assignments. At the Rifkins I had no table on which to study. The only furniture in our small room was a pull-out bed positioned against one wall. I complained to Mutti. In comparison to Rose Cottage and our other lodgings in East New York, the Rifkin household did not seem to value schoolwork; it was always a problem to use the kitchen table. Within a couple weeks Mutti appeared with a small, square-shaped table that just fit; it also had a shelf for storing books and papers. Somehow she had managed to carry it onto the buses and subways that brought her to Miller Avenue each week.

She also arranged for an alternative Shabbes afternoon. We had distant relatives from Hamburg-Altona who had begun settling in eastern Brownsville in 1938. On many a Shabbes we walked some twenty-five blocks, past the black neighborhood around Rockaway Avenue, to the Glücksmanns, where a religiously observant spirit reigned. In the midst of the Depression they were trying to prevent Harry, the youngest of three children, from abandoning Jewish traditions too quickly. Manfred and I grew close to Cilli, a wonderfully warm and strong woman, to Harry, and to his older brother, Arnold.[6] Arnold and Harry became big brothers. We talked, walked, ate peanuts and raisins, learned how to play chess, gained an introduction to Harry's Brownsville teenage youth culture, and heard a lot about Arnold's work as an egg candler, a specialty he had acquired from his father, a longtime grocery merchant in Altona. When Arnold married, his wife Helen became a kind of big sister, especially after he and Harry went off to war. She moved in with Cilli and shared some of Arnold's letters with us.

The clash in values with Mrs. Rifkin exploded in 1943, just before Passover. In past years when Mutti could not leave work,

Manfred and I had spent the seder evenings with the Kormans on the Lower East Side or at this or that table among the Engelberg clan living in East New York.[7] Now, together with Mutti, we expected to make a seder on Miller Avenue. Mrs. Rifkin had initially agreed, but a few days before the start of Passover the Missus announced in her tense and shrill voice: "No. No! No Pesach with my sons in the army." This was done at the last minute, when it was too late to make other arrangements. Yet there it was, the real possibility that we would not have a seder, our first with all three of us present. In Nadnia it was possible. In Talaton it was possible. On Miller Avenue it was impossible because World War II had at last penetrated Mrs. Rifkin's soul.

Mutti seemed to respond to Mrs. Rifkin with more discipline than I could muster, perhaps because she fully appreciated what it meant to be a refugee in the Jewish world on which we so depended. She had wrestled with many New York Jews who tried to impose their will. It began shortly after her arrival in New York. While she was asking a policeman for directions in her German-accented, fractured English, a stranger interrupted in Yiddish: "Don't tell her. She is German." An East European Jew, rightfully bitter at the treatment German Jews had usually meted out to East European Jews during the vast emigrations from Russia and Poland, was taking his personal revenge out on a daughter of East European Jews who long before had settled in the Rhineland. But he did not know that and, besides, it might not have made any difference anyway. His need to take revenge on anyone who sounded like German Jews—which for him meant the types turning Manhattan's Washington Heights neighborhood into the Fourth Reich—was simply an ordinary fact of life.

At Jewish welfare agencies and at the homes of relatives Mutti had to beg. When I became a Bar Mitzvah, she had no money for a suit. How could I not have a suit! The hand-me-down clothing did not fit. Pictures from those years show us wearing oversized pants, with tightly cinched belts creating unshapely pleats between the waist and the crotch. She received five dollars from HIAS and managed to find a new suit at May's department store in Brooklyn. When the deal with the Petrovers turned ugly, it also revealed her financial circumstances. Mutti did not have the money to pay her debts promptly, and the Petrovers pressed hard, either because they were also hurting or because they just wanted their money.

Starting in December 1940, they sent one reminder letter after another to the uncle who, by virtue of his affidavit for Mutti, was legally liable. John Petrover was brutally frank: "On September 10, 1940, Mrs. Korman brought her two boys over to my house, claiming nobody [sic] of her relatives would take them, and I agreed to keep them against payment of $60 a month for board. Finally I reduced the board price for the month of November to $55 with the understanding of a final payoff until Dec. 1. The older boy Gerd was behaving himself in such a bad and fresh way toward my wife that we did not [want to] keep him any longer."[8] By February Mr. Petrover threatened legal action. He rejected Mutti's offer to pay him five dollars a month. "Could you take care of the board of other people's children, after you have been in this country one year? I am not able to do this, as I am a man who has to work very hard [to provide] for the living of my own family. Now I am up against it and need the money myself in full immediately." Petrover wanted his money and suggested that the uncle accept payments of five dollars a month. "After all, your niece brought the children right away to you on their arrival from the boat. How could you," he asked with justification, "send the boys with Mrs. Korman by your son-in-law, Mr. Rappaport, to my house at $60 board a month if there is no money to pay for? The responsibility is fully on your side. Otherwise why did not you accommodate the children right away with some one of your own family, as it is done now, after I refused to keep the boys any longer?" Mutti's uncle sent that letter to her with a note saying he wanted to clear the account. "As you have stated to me that you only owe him $35, please send me a copy of your figures." That should have been the end of it, but granddaughter Beatrice intervened by adding a postscript to the uncle's handwritten note: "Received your air mail letter— Grandpa is very sick and can't do anything for you."[9]

Yet Mutti never turned bitter toward New York Jews in general. She never forgot that after the stranger had spoken to the policeman, that officer answered her in Yiddish and gently told her where to go. The warmth and love of the Oelbaums, and especially of the Kormans on the Lower East Side, sustained her; the latter were Pappi's relatives from his hometown of Narol, whom she had not met before coming to New York. And even the Rifkins, despite all the problems, were for Mutti angels of mercy who allowed her to earn a living with a sense of assurance that all was well with her boys. Besides, she probably understood Mrs. Rifkin at a deeper level. They both had sons. So she found another solution in Great Neck, where a friend offered Mutti the use of her apartment.

As we had done in Nadnia and Talaton, we improvised; all three of us were now quite experienced in temporary shelter living. This time it was also exciting because Manfred and I could really help Mutti with the preparations for making the apartment fit for a kosher Passover. We knew what to do. While she was on her job nearby, we scrubbed and covered most of the friend's year-round dishes and cutlery, cleaned inside cupboards and all the food-serving surfaces we could identify. Then we unwrapped the few new dishes we had bought and put them into their proper place. Next came the stove and general kitchen utensils, but these presented an additional challenge. After preparing the stove, we had to purify the pots, pans, and cutlery according to a prescribed ritual.

Using a match, we lit each of the four top burners. When we finally located the jet for the pilot light, we reached deep into the oven with a lighted, rolled-up piece of newspaper, ignited the pilot, and turned on the oven. As each of the burners blazed at their highest temperatures, Manfred and I had to decide how long to let them burn. We thought ten minutes was long enough, but to be on the safe side we allowed them all to burn for half an hour. Now we were ready to look for an immersion container, that is, for the biggest metal pot in the apartment—and for a stone.

We found the pot in a lower cupboard and the stone outside, a nice smooth one in the shape of a small Idaho potato. I filled the pot, up to the three-quarter mark, placed it on a front burner, and turned the gas flame way up. I placed the stone into the oven and lit it. As the water in the pot began to heat up, we kept on checking the stone to see if it was red-hot yet. I needed to know because I had been told by someone whose name I had forgotten that it was necessary to place a glowing stone into the pot of boiling water before the dunking of the utensils could begin.

When the moment arrived, I was at a loss as to how to transfer the stone. I recall the splash the stone made as I let go of it but can't recall how that glowing stone in a stranger's kitchen was transferred. I know we went on to make the utensils fit for Passover by dunking them in the boiling water. Once Mutti arrived, she completed the seder preparations. I know that afterward the three of us celebrated our seder alone, conscious that it might be foreshadowing future Passovers without Pappi or, as we hoped, that it would be the first step in the reunification of the family.

8

Strangers also helped celebrate Manfred's Bar Mitzvah in a spectacular fashion: our financially strapped synagogue used the event as a fund-raiser. It was a remarkable affair, especially given the fact that it was held in our refugee shelter on Miller Avenue. As was the case at my Bar Mitzvah, the congregation also turned to a well-to-do family for a special contribution, but this time its leader used the Bar Mitzvah for their congregation's larger fiscal purposes. The Rabbi and his assistants trained Manny so that he would be able to perform his ritual obligations with precision, which he did beautifully; he even managed to control his Zbaszyn stutter. Friends and relatives came, as did strangers, all of whom heard Manfred chant from the Torah and listened to the fund-raising speeches of special guests. It was a gala affair.

Even as they helped us in so many ways, Jews in the neighborhood and in the congregation never let us forget that we were refugees, children of a single working mother, unfortunates comparable to orphans or children of a poor widow. It was a complicated relationship, one that had led to the tensions between the Rifkins and myself. Our neighbors helped on terms familiar to them: they knew how to assist orphans, the widow, and her children. We, however, did not see ourselves in those terms and they recognized that we did not fit their model of the unfortunate poor.

On the one hand, Manfred and I benefited from a patronizing attitude because neighbors arranged for us to earn needed pocket money. Early on I became the delivery boy for Mr. Epstein's grocery store. Rolls and milk were delivered throughout the neighborhood between half past five and half past six in the morning. At Passover time Manfred and I also earned tip money delivering orders for another, larger store nearby.

On the other hand, especially with respect to synagogue affairs, we were never allowed to forget our station. I remember feeling hurt during Manfred's Bar Mitzvah celebration. I had accepted the role of squatter during High Holy Day services because I had no choice but to sit where there happened to be an empty seat. I remembered how I sat next to Pappi in Hamburg's great Bornplatz, or in the one-room makeshift synagogue in Nadnia. I hated to squat! On a Friday night or Shabbes, when so many synagogue members stayed at home, Manfred and I could sit just about anywhere without concern of being bumped. On the High Holy Days it was different. Neither Mutti nor the Rifkins came, so that meant we had no adults whose ticket or reserved seat we could squeeze into or claim as our own. We had to sit wherever there was room and be prepared to get bumped, sometimes as often as two or three times within half an hour.

At Manfred's Bar Mitzvah celebration the powers that be also bumped me. Once we left the sanctuary, it became obvious that Mutti had paid the bill by becoming a guest at her own party. She had been permitted to invite some friends and relatives but had no say about all other arrangements, including the head table. As Mutti and I approached, both of us planning to sit next to Manfred, someone waved me to one of the round tables in the center of the large room. I broke into tears as I stared at Mutti, Manfred, and the visiting rabbis in their black garb, beards, skullcaps, and all.

That was in December 1944, by which time Mutti had come to live in our neighborhood. She had quit Great Neck, turned herself into a practical baby nurse—a registered practical aide to mothers with newborn infants—and was finding sleep-in work all over the city. Each job lasted about two weeks. In between assignments she'd be home, at 412 Miller Avenue, just down the block, in a room rented from Mrs. Berger, the sister of Dr. Anderman and mother of Morty, Manny's best friend. Mutti became a fixture on the street where we lived, especially for the postman, for whom she always waited in the hope that he had mail from Holland. She was a good-looking woman, just over forty, petite, with graying black hair and flashing dark eyes whose glance was sufficient to restrain us in our wilder moments. Everybody knew how hard she worked to make ends meet, increasingly less as a European and more as a proud New Yorker, accent and all, an independent woman making it in New York.

She had somehow persuaded me that Pappi would arrive someday. Since the United States had become an enemy to Nazi-occupied Holland, we had no way of knowing that he was alive. The news out of Europe was horrific, especially if, like Mutti, one read *Aufbau* and heard news secondhand from those reading the Yiddish dailies, such as the *Forward* or the *Morning Journal*. Mutti, however, would not give up hope, and neither did I, even though I was conscious of having lost "something." When we were "swept apart," I wrote in 1944, "something was swept out of me and God knows when it will return. I can't explain what that something is as I don't know myself. I feel different, though, and have felt different since the day I left." When I turned sixteen, I told Mutti in German: "Six years ago the world looked different. Then we had our own home, made a good living, and in general fared well. Now . . . we stand in a very different world. No home, no family. But despite all, we have something, namely, hope and health, that no one can take away. Yes, liebe Mutti, now there is a tragedy in the world which will leave a long night. We must hold ourselves hale and hearty for the glorious day when the sun will break through the clouds, the world again radiates with beauty and goodness, when our father will return and all Jews will find their home."

When I wrote that letter almost seven weeks had passed since the successful invasion of Normandy. In the next months we studied battle maps with mounting anticipation, paying particular attention to General Montgomery's forces, which, after the Battle of the Bulge, pushed into southern Holland. Westerbork was not far from Groningen and near Assen, in northeast Holland. This area was attacked later, near the end of the war.

On April 12, the day President Roosevelt died, Canadians engaged German tank units around the Orange Canal, just a few miles from the camp. After crossing it, they headed for Westerbork, the camp and the village after which it had been named. Some in the camp had ventured to the outside perimeter and now rushed back with the news: "The Canadians. The Canadians are coming." To some they looked like "a moving beehive, then another, then another. There were tanks packed with people who had encountered them first." They came into the camp, celebrated the liberation with about a thousand inmates, and—according to one of the liberated—upon discovering that these inmates were organized and healthy, concentrated on looking for German collaborators. However, Rabbi Samuel Cass, the army chaplain from Toronto who entered the camp eight days later, made himself available to Westerbork's Jews, who were eager to connect with the larger Jewish world, especially events in Palestine. He also circulated among the former inmates, offering to send news of their liberation to loved ones.[1]

We were in school, but Mutti happened to be on Miller Avenue when she saw the mailman coming down the block. He was a few hours early because it was only around 1 P.M. Suddenly she realized he was coming straight toward her. Holding something in his raised right hand, he said: "I hope it's what you've been waiting for, good news from your husband." Then he turned around to walk back some ten blocks before resuming his normal delivery route. Mutti opened the official-looking letter and read that Pappi was alive! The whole neighborhood heard her cries of joy.

In the next few months we heard from Pappi often in letters, postcards, and much-anticipated monthly international phone calls. The first one was truly exciting: Manfred and I could hardly remember the sound of his voice and Pappi had to get used to ours, which had deepened because of adolescence. Besides, we had never spoken to each other in English.

He reached out in so many different ways, demonstrating how dear we were to him in his few sharply etched memories. On December 23, 1945, his birthday letter when Manfred turned fourteen said it all. First he apologized for having missed Manfred's birthday by a few days. Then he reminisced, the seven years running together:

How many years has it been since we were all together celebrating your birthday? Actually, it was in 1937 because by 1938 we were already in Zbaszyn and there it was impossible to celebrate. I believe you felt those days most intensely. You could not find your place. Everybody tossed you about, and when you fell ill it took so long for me to obtain permission to bring you into the private home where I was staying. My heart bled, but there was nothing I could do. Fortunately, when we came to Nadnia we were together, and we had a few good weeks; the walks with you and Gerd, in sunshine or rain, were exciting and lovely. One retains only flashes of memory. There is another such moment that I recall. When you had recovered from scarlet fever in the Eppendorfer Hospital [Hamburg], still pretty small, not quite with it, you immediately became interested in [our] car. In the evening I usually brought it to a garage and took you along. We drove in, put the car into its stall, and closed it. And now came the moment I still have in my mind's eye. I see you in your Loden coat, with your somewhat yellowish looking face, and because of the color, your especially big-looking eyes, kneeling on the ground, peering through the slit to make certain that the car is still in the stall. Convinced, you and I went home. You were reassured but you regretted having to leave.

That letter was in German, but he also wrote in English, a fluent English that reminded us of his studies in Hamburg. This still surprised us. After all these years, how was he able to remember his English in a camp in Holland? In one card on July 1, 1945, addressed to his "Dear boys," he inquired about our schooling, given that I was seventeen years old. He also asked: "Are you already U.S. subjects?," broaching a topic much on our family's collective mind. Pappi and Mutti were already involved with postwar immigration clerks trying to get Pappi to us in America.

Mutti had never stopped trying. Since 1939, when Pappi arrived in Holland, Dutch and American clerks had fingered his files.[2] Periodically she even turned to Albert Einstein, the famous but always responsive fellow refugee, and asked him to use the power of his name on her behalf—all to no avail.[3] However, in 1945 Pappi's chances were much better even though antisemitism continued to inform congressional policymakers and State Department officials.[4] In the fall she prepared and submitted an Affidavit of Support of her own and managed to persuade an Engelberg relative to provide a supplementary affidavit. As a baby nurse, Mutti could demonstrate that she had a skilled occupation and worked with a respectable agency: "She is a good nurse and very well liked. She earns seventy dollars . . . per week," reported the head of the Star Registry for Nurses in a notarized statement. "She has been continuously employed since November 1944 except for 5 weeks' vacation." Mutti could also prove that her bank account had around eight hundred dollars and that she held four hundred in war bonds.[5] For his part, Morris, the son-in-law of Wolf Engelberg, one of Mutti's few senior relatives who cared about us, supported her affidavit from the earnings and investments of his fur business, which had annual sales of more than one and a half million dollars.[6]

By the end of January 1946 she had succeeded. A form letter from the assistant commissioner of the Immigration and Naturalization Service informed her: "The petition was approved for the relative Osias Korman and forwarded . . . to the appropriate American consulate abroad, where such relative(s) should apply for the visa(s)."[7] The next and final step had to be taken in Amsterdam, where the American consulate was expected to issue a nonquota visa to Pappi.

Jewish clerks also sounded familiar echoes from the past. It was again a matter of money, money the committees wanted and that my parents did not have and could not obtain from relatives. On March 19, 1946, a few months before Pappi's departure from Holland, Ann S. Petluck, of the National Refugee Service, wrote Mutti about Case #41582, seemingly suggesting that her agency could hold up Pappi's crossing: "We are writing on behalf of your husband, who is interested in entering the United States for permanent residence." Then the director turned to the heart of the letter, claiming that Amsterdam was requesting that "we discuss with you your activity on behalf of your husband . . . your ability to help your husband so that his plans for immigration may materialize in the near future." Fortunately, the indebtedness for the ticket did not interfere with Pappi's departure, but some of the Joint's different committees kept at it, trying to get their money back for Pappi's transportation costs. Periodically Mutti would receive reminder letters. In August 1947 Amsterdam insisted it had "expended a total of $228." As far as that office was concerned, Amsterdam would be reimbursed. A unit of the Brooklyn section of the National Council of Jewish Women, wrote Mutti on August 5, 1947, wanting to know what "plan" Mutti had in place to meet "the request of the committee abroad."

Finally Pappi stepped in, although I never did learn how the spent $228 was resolved. Years later it occurred to Mutti that we really did not owe the Joint anything at all since, following liberation, Pappi had worked for the Joint in Amsterdam and had chaperoned five younger passengers when they sailed to the United States.[8] For its part the Joint had kept its books up to date. When Pappi was a passenger aboard the *St. Louis*, $710 had been deposited for him in an account held by the National Refugee Service. "With the depositor's approval," the Joint's committee in Holland received $519.86 to cover Pappi's refugee-related expenses there. The depositor had "authorized the National Refugee Service to purchase tickets for you and your two children." However, as in spring 1940, Manfred and I could not sail with Mutti; $234 remained in the account. When we did sail in the fall of that year, the tickets cost $186.84. According to the Joint's reckoning, it had spent $940.70 on our family. In this later accounting the $228 for Pappi's ticket had obviously disappeared![9]

As the day of Pappi's arrival approached, it dawned on me that our coming home again would also bring the unexpected. We in New York all knew each other, but how would Pappi relate to us and we to him? We had been grazing in so many different fields for almost eight years, always hoping to bring an end to it. Now, in 1946, when we were about to reunite, the family of my dreams remained hidden. I was a teenager with a maturing sense of his own privacy, involving sex and girlfriends, but not conscious of the intimate feelings of mother and father as husband and wife.

Since our separation on the third day of Passover at the Zbaszyn railway station, we had each held part of ourselves in shadow, somehow shielding it against outside pressures. Pappi's presence was always available for the day fast approaching. However, each of us had changed a lot. Was I still my father's son after more than five years in East New York? I was now eighteen, about to enter my senior year at Brooklyn Tech, a staunch Zionist hearing Palestine's battle cry, an acclaimed soccer player, and a Yankee fan cheering for his first American heroes: DiMaggio and Rizzuto. Mutti had heard of them, sort of, but Pappi? He didn't know any of them, whether the sport was baseball, softball, or stickball. Likewise Glen Miller and Artie Shaw. I also was a not so observant a Jew. How observant was he? Had the camp experiences changed his beliefs?

So what kind of paternal authority would I—could I—grant him? I had been a kind of stand-in father for Manfred, who was now turning fourteen, a high school student at nearby Thomas

Jefferson. He was older than I had been when Pappi had left for Hamburg from the Zbaszyn station, where the previous October, at Neu Benschen, the Germans had stripped him of his parental authority over me.

Everything would be different. Since arriving in America, Mutti and both of us had grown closer, this despite the fact that we had lived in different locations. I had wanted to go to Palestine, but on Miller Avenue no one seemed interested in the fight for Eretz Yisrael; they were too busy making a living while coping with returning soldiers or with the loss of loved ones. But I also knew I was not going to abandon Mutti and Manfred, surely not now, when Pappi was coming. And Mutti and Pappi? They had been separated by so much more than six years. She had become an independent New Yorker responsible for supporting her family; she was now in charge, trying to figure out where to house and feed us on her income alone, at least until she had helped Pappi find a job. Given the web of information and misinformation about displaced persons, one question none of us in New York dared verbalize about Pappi, who had been liberated from Germany's terrifying camps, was: Who was he, this long-time prisoner of Westerbork?

After we learned that Pappi had his visa and ticket, first things did have to come first.[10] By mid-July we had to find an apartment where we could live as a united family. I say we, but it was Mutti who did it all. Manfred and I were schoolboys, with part-time jobs and the obligations that bind teenagers to their friends and acquaintances. She decided to look for an apartment on or around Miller Avenue, where we had supporting friends and relatives and helpful neighbors, merchants, and religious leaders. She also looked in our neighborhood because she assumed that she'd find an apartment within the right price range. Her weekly salary was about forty dollars,[11] while Manfred's and my contribution came to about fifteen dollars, making available about sixty to seventy dollars a month for rent.

In 1946 in postwar Brooklyn's East New York, on the streets where we lived, an empty apartment for a family of four did not exist—at least Mutti did not find one that she could afford. What she did find was disappointment, not unlike the feeling Manfred and I felt when we learned that once again we would be living with strangers in a temporary shelter, apart from Mutti. She found a sublet at 373 Miller Avenue, on the top floor of one of those walk-up tenement houses that marked Miller Avenue between Belmont and Pitkin as a lower-class street in comparison with the adjacent block we lived on, at 392 and 412. Some advantages were obvious: the sublet was big enough; it had sufficient rooms, including a kosher kitchen; was furnished; and was seemingly affordable. Its disadvantage was also obvious: it came with elderly Mr. Krisinsky, our landlord. We would have to feed him at dinnertime, share his kitchen and bathroom, and clean up after him, something I never took into account from his perspective.

At the end of June Mutti reluctantly rented it. We would not be home alone. She did not know anything about Mr. Krisinsky, his health, his habits, or his appetite. The apartment was hot in summer even with a fan and open windows. She also worried about the comparison we would each make: Mutti was vacating a lovely room in Mrs. Berger's house on the better block; Manfred and I had been living in a cleaner and well-kept apartment house on the corner; and Pappi was leaving rooms on Stadium Weg, near Amsterdam's Konzertgebau. In some fashion all of us remembered something of the apartment on Behnstrasse 5— especially Mutti. When pressed, she could recall details about the furnishings, such as the two carpets, the runner, the pots and frying pans in the kitchen, the tea service, and the children's desk. Mutti rented the sublet because she was convinced each of us would somehow manage to make do with what we had, including old man Krisinsky.

In the following days, as Pappi sailed on the merchant ship *City of Alma* from Rotterdam toward Mobile, Alabama, we prepared the apartment. After we brought in what little furniture and kitchen supplies we owned or could afford to buy, Manfred went to work on the windows, even leaning out over the ledge to view the street traffic the way we used to do in Hamburg. During the week of Pappi's arrival, we bought some nonperishable food for the cupboard and stocked the small refrigerator. Fortunately for us, just down the street we had our friendly butcher, grocer, and vegetable man, each of whom customarily carried accounts for weeks on end.

9

Pappi's cable from Mobile arrived on Friday, July 19. Together with his younger orphaned DPs, he had arrived at State Docks around 9 P.M. the evening before, excited and proud, but also sobered by a scary experience when the ship had called at its first American port, Poco Grande, Florida. Some of the crew had been given shore leave, and Pappi was allowed to take his first walk on U.S. soil: Florida was where he should have ended up after Cuba had sent the *St. Louis* out of Havana. Suddenly, around 11:30 P.M., he had to deal with the curses and threatening body language of a drunken, antisemitic sailor returning to the ship.

In Mobile all six passengers met local reporters who were eager to inform readers about the gruesome experiences of the "first cargo of war orphans" that had arrived in the city. Meanwhile the Mobile Council of Jewish Women arranged for their layover before sending them by train to their various American destinations.[1] Pappi and one of his charges, Frank Aaron, were scheduled to leave Saturday on an overnight train to New York—at least that's what the cable said: ARRIVED SAFELY. WILL BE IN NEW YORK SUNDAY MORNING 7:00 PENNSYL-VANIA STATION. Odd, I remember thinking to myself, that he signed it Osias. Mutti had always called him Max.

Osias came to us with a Westerbork past about which we knew nothing. He carried it in his heart and mind and in the files of his luggage. Having been one of the first refugee internees sent by the Dutch to help establish Westerbork, a single person without any family, he was chosen by a camp committee to join the second group of such singles to complete the organization and construction of the new camp. He also did what he had done in Nadnia, namely, assume responsibility for making sure that fellow Jews had the organizations and institutions that tradition required.

In an ironic twist of fortune, he came to be identified as a so-called St. Louis Baron. He happened to be on the *St. Louis,* with its complement of middle- and upper-middle-class German Jews, because he had been deported as a Polish Jew; he just happened to be back in Hamburg the exact month the *St. Louis* opportunity occurred. He was not a German Jew, nor was he part of the senior German Jewish junta. This group served as a Westerbork Jewish Council in a spirit similar to the coerced "administrative cooperation" by which the Dutch banks, civil service, and railways dealt with German policies of occupation. However, by virtue of his *St. Louis* experience, Osias, a German-speaking former longtime resident of Germany, was one of 181 passengers who joined with other German Jewish refugees in building Westerbork from the bottom up. As such, he was a St. Louis Baron because as a group they had been in the camp since 1939, and because he became a barracks leader and held other positions in a camp administration developed first by the Dutch government and then, after the invasion, as part of the command structure of the German government of occupation. In other words, from early on in the history of Westerbork, he was part of a permanent internal administrative cadre of senior camp inmates—some, like him, without any family in the camp—who were exempt from deportation orders long enough to experience liberation in Westerbork.

Osias and his fellow prisoners did not know about the larger German scheme that made Westerbork a transit camp par excellence in a huge prison system, slaughter houses and all. Even after July 1942, when barbed wire surrounded the refugee camp and it became a prison camp under direct German rule, the camp usually succeeded in functioning as a lure—attracting desperate Jews who had been exposed to increasingly repressive practices and deportation roundups—and a mirage—convincing prisoners that they were part of a wartime complex using forced labor from all over Europe.

They could not help but know that Dutch and German railway schedules dictated the rhythm of each inmate's life in the camp. Trains brought many into the camp and trains took many out of it. After July 1942, on any given day there were thousands of prisoners—almost all Dutch Jews. Each train, usually consisting

Pappi at Camp Westerbork in Holland, ca. 1942–43. This detail of a group picture taken by German officials is in a German photo album now located at Yad Vashem, Jerusalem, Israel.

of freight cars, regularly took hundreds to the east. Osias and many others suspected that the transports were taking Westerborkers to terrible forced-labor camps, where they would meet their deaths from illness, hunger, and exhaustion.

They also heard rumors of gassing, although that truth about the Holocaust—as we later came to call the catastrophe—he learned only after liberation, when Dutch authorities resumed command of the camp and retained him as a barracks leader for survivors like himself. Surely by April 21, when Rabbi Cass arrived, he had learned about the Final Solution, which in Auschwitz, Bergen-Belsen, Sobibor, or Theresienstadt accounted for more than a hundred thousand Westerbork lives.

It was from that perspective, living with the Westerbork past, that he was now arriving at Pennsylvania Station. He had escaped the worst of overcrowded public barracks life. He had participated in its cultural programs, where he continued his study of English. He had stayed off the transports. Osias never saw death camps or Theresienstadt.

Among the prisoners with whom he was forced to live and work, he retained the respect and friendship of those who had also been liberated in Westerbork or, more often than not, in Bergen-Belsen or Auschwitz. They knew what he had tried to accomplish with whatever authority had been granted him, namely, to sustain Jewish religious and cultural values, especially among the young, to keep prisoners on work details, to do anything and everything to keep them off the godforsaken transports. To them he was one of the "Barons," but he was also a kind of Jewish hero figure.

At Westerbork he was grateful for his deep friendship with Etty Hillesum, who always called him Osias, an act of endearment that gave new meaning to a name only government officials used to refer to him. In Westerbork she displayed the strength and courage necessary to maintain contact with the Dutch resistance and to stand up as a righteous creature trying to salvage shards of humanity. Pappi had letters from her dated 1943, when she was twenty-nine, as well as several photographs; that was the year she joined the transports to meet the killers at Auschwitz.

The friendship dated from her arrival from Amsterdam. By then he was a barracks leader, had private quarters, and could

Etty Hillesum, ca. 1942–43.

share that precious private space with her and her suitcase. She had come as a representative of Amsterdam's Jewish Council, expecting to liaise between the city organization and the camp. In August 1942 she came twice, once staying for four weeks, when their initial meetings turned into a close personal relationship. From her perspective they were special comrades with connections to other good comrades. Etty distinguished this group from other Jews in the Westerbork-Amsterdam network by observing that others often thought about fellow Jews as if they were purchasing a tube of toothpaste.

In their comradeship, Jews like themselves sought to transcend acts of Nazi humiliation, pride either of German or Dutch origin, and feelings of class rank; they also tried to place human needs above order and efficiency. That comradeship, however, did not prevent its members from enjoying or seeking special privileges. As an agent of the Jewish Council, Etty could travel in and out of Westerbork when her health permitted. As a St. Louis Baron, Pappi could enter Amsterdam; he had been issued official passes, some of which he saved among his papers. In other words, Pappi and Etty held privileged positions and could offer some protection to friends and relatives in addition to themselves.

Etty described such efforts while attempting to keep her parents and brother off the trains. It was July 1943, a horrible month in the history of the camp. The mounting "suspense every week," waiting to see who would go, was dreadful. "It didn't bother me so much before, because I had accepted the fact that I would be going to Poland. But living in fear for your loved ones, knowing then an infinitely long martyrdom is in store for them while your own life is relatively idyllic, is something few can bear." On a day when she was trying to do something she had never done before, namely, taking "a hand in 'fixing' it" so that a special friend among the comrades would be kept off the transport, she sensed the "underworld" involved in all the selections. "I don't know how it all fits together; I don't think its a savory story. Anyway, I trudged around the whole day, while my parents were entrusted to Kormann's watchful eye and to the staff of the Jewish Council, who assured me that everything would be all right this time." On another day she wrote: "Slowly but steadily the camp is being sucked dry. Without some miracle from the outside, it will be over in a week or two. What we really want is to get Mischa [her brother], who is determined to stick with his parents and face certain doom, away from here." She realized how hard it had become: "The worst part is that you are able to do so much less for your people than they expect. Six months ago it would probably still have been fairly simple to keep them back here and make them feel quite at home, but I am becoming more helpless all the time."

Things got progressively worse. "A complete madhouse here; we shall have to feel ashamed of it for three hundred years. The Dienstleiters [Jewish section heads] themselves now have to draw up the transport lists. Meetings, panic—it's all horrible." In the midst of this day of transport-related terror, the camp commandant ordered those same section heads to attend "the first night of a cabaret, which is being put on here." Thus, that same night they had to dress up and pretend they were enjoying a concert. "I wasn't there myself," she wrote, "but Kormann just told me about it, adding, 'This whole business is slowly driving me to the edge of despair.'"

In the end, both their efforts did not keep Etty's parents and brother off the train. Nor could Etty stay. All along she had insisted that she was not going to leave with her loved ones. "I shan't go, I just can't. It is easier to pray for someone from a long distance than to see him suffer by your side. It is not fear of Poland that keeps me from going along with my parents, but fear of seeing them suffer." When she joined her parents and brother on the train, the choice had not been hers. It was in the hands of Germans, who were shipping her to Auschwitz.

Osias Korman grieved. With her letters and photographs always close at hand, he shielded his treasure, the fruits of a short, intense, inspired friendship. His friend—he was forty-five and she was twenty-nine at the time—was a woman who had confided to her diary: "I would rather be alone [than marry] and there for everyone"; a woman who realized that she "pursued" her "own pleasure too much"; someone "who was so ready, of an evening on the heath, to gaze into a friendly pair of eyes"; a comrade who asked God to stand up for human goodness in the face of evil.

He also shared his special camp space and position with others, including some of Etty's friends from Amsterdam, who were shipped into the camp, as well as with Berlin's well-known Fritz and Liesel Levy and their small children. Following the liberation, Osias and Liesel bumped into each other on a street in Amsterdam, stunned to find the other among the living; she and the little ones had survived Bergen-Belsen. For about a year they helped each other and her fatherless children find their way; her children called him "Kor."

Still, Pappi was overwhelmed by the conflicting tensions resulting from his Westerbork past. He and Eric Cohn and some other camp friends had frequently discussed the possibility of permanently disabling the efficient bureaucracy of which they were a part. However, in the midst of war—the imposed isolation and ignorance; the seeming inactivity of Dutch resistance fighters and of railway workers in Westerbork and in the larger Dutch transport net—there seemed little justification for inflicting the additional pain of chaos upon themselves and others. He had been successful and lucky in staying off the transports, although more than once he had come close to volunteering.

He had sought to protect his soul in the folds of his Judaism and Zionism and even tried to extend it to those about him; he recalled that on one Passover he and a few others actually baked matzos. Even so, during most of his Westerbork internment he was convinced that he'd never again see his family. Sometimes he let himself hope that perhaps there was a chance of surviving after all. When the bitter truth about Auschwitz emerged, his doubts and recriminations mingled with memories. He wrestled with Judaism's God. In November 1945 he did not think about the "death" of God, did not invoke Jeremiah's indictment ("You have killed without mercy"), did not demand to put God on trial, and did not speculate about the God who had hidden his face. Instead, he adopted chapter 9 of Ecclesiastes as his guide to help him understand why God's justice is not human justice: "All things come alike to all: there is one event to the righteous and to the wicked; to the good and to the clean and to the unclean; to him who sacrifices, and to him who does not sacrifice: as is the good, so is the sinner . . . There is one event for all: yea, also the heart of the sons of men is full of evil, madness is in their heart while they live. And after that they go to the dead." Max Korman was convinced that Jews had experienced an evil fashioned by human hands. Pappi also brought with him nervous tensions, depressions, constant nightmares, and the fear of sudden death.[2]

We were busy chatting with the Weichmanns when the train arrived. They had come for Frankie, a sister's son who was now an orphan. The Weichmanns had fled Germany when his past positions in the Weimar government and Social Democratic Party placed him at risk. In New York Herbert had become an accountant, but he and his wife were seriously thinking of returning to postwar Germany and joining old friends now struggling to govern Hamburg. Would Frankie go with them? That was the unresolved question when the train arrived on the platform to our right.

"There he is," Mutti called out as a short man stepped off, turned, and deliberately walked toward us. I don't remember our embrace. We hurried to keep up with the porter who was transporting Pappi's luggage on his cart. He introduced himself to Frankie's new parents while we said hello to Frankie. Then everybody exchanged good-byes. Next we headed for the exit from Penn Station, hailed an expensive Yellow Cab, and clambered into one with two jump seats facing the back. We were together, sitting next to each other, holding hands, stroking cheeks, talking, crying, playing tour guide for our immigrant Pappi, who spoke a beautiful English! His blue-gray eyes still peered through steel-rimmed eyeglass frames, which he pushed up along the bridge of his nose with his bent index finger every so often.

We drove south to Manhattan Bridge, crossed over into Brooklyn, and then headed for Atlantic Avenue, with its Long Island Railroad elevated tracks. We didn't know the neighborhoods, so we could only comment on those street names that reminded us of subway stops, which signaled the difference between home turf and the outsider's territory. Until we reached Brownsville, we were in "their" country. But when Atlantic crossed Saratoga Avenue we could tell Pappi about the Glücksmanns, Cilli and Harry, and Arnold and Helen, who lived south of Atlantic Avenue.

As we approached East New York, Pappi's face darkened. Perhaps I had not noticed it before, but now it was obvious. He was troubled about the neighborhood in which we lived. The closer we came to Miller Avenue, the more detailed and enthusiastic our descriptions, the darker grew his countenance. By the time the driver had turned onto Miller Avenue itself, Pappi was silent. So were we, not knowing what to say or make of his reactions. At number 373 we sang out: "We're home, we're home," and in no time at all we brought Pappi's luggage up to our apartment. "Hello Mr. Krisinsky" meant good-bye to grazing days in barren fields.

Later in the day we walked along our side of Miller Avenue, crossed Belmont and Miller, and stood in front of number 392. We showed Pappi the corner stores and then climbed up the stairs to say hello to the Rifkins, the Gussows, and a few others in the apartment house. Afterward we visited with Mrs. Berger and the Andermans, greeted friends and acquaintances on the street, and, before turning back to number 373, turned onto Sutter Avenue to show Pappi our favorite movie house.

In the next few days there were evening visits to relatives, to Brandel and others belonging to the extended Engelberg clan, but none was as dramatic as the meeting with Shimen Korman in Brownsville's Prospect Place Market. Manfred and I took Pappi by subway to a place neither of us had seen before. Shimen's instructions were simple and direct: "Once you step into the market, just keep on walking straight ahead. Try to come around eleven in the morning. Don't worry. I'll see you coming."

The three of us entered the market not knowing what to expect: so many strange sounds and smells. Shimen was a gruff and unpredictable man. When we sat down to eat at his table the first time and didn't take big portions, he yelled: "Who tells you to eat?" However, on another occasion when we did take big portions he bellowed: "All you do is eat. You come here and all you do is eat." He also drank a lot of whiskey without seeming to get drunk. He dressed in such funny ways, especially on those rare occasions when he wore a tie. His appearance was always outlandish, with nothing seeming to match, especially the same shirt we usually saw him wearing. He had never said much about Pappi, so I was uncertain that he remembered him when he occasionally reminisced about his many dead Narol relatives. I thought he was Pappi's second cousin, with whom he had not spent much time together.

And now here was short-sleeved Shimen coming toward us. He looked big, tall, broad-shouldered. By comparison, Pappi—and, for that matter, Manfred and I—seemed small, even tiny. Then an odd thing happened. The closer Shimen approached, the less I became aware of the market's sounds and smells. He and Pappi were moving in slow motion, Pappi a step ahead of us and Shimen closing in. When they were within touching distance, Shimen stretched out his arms and lifted Pappi high into the air before lowering him gently and giving him a bear hug, sobbing tears of joy for all to see and hear. In the next months he did everything he could to help Pappi become a salesman again, including offering him an interest-free eight hundred-dollar loan to buy a new car, a two-door Ford with a sharply sloping back roof and no heater.

The purchase of that car was symbolic: we three old timers were making it possible for Pappi to again become the independent head of our household. The car, arranging contacts for work, dealing with Jewish agencies—those were in Mutti's hands. Yet in no time at all English-speaking Pappi, with the help of his own network of old friends now living in New York, was doing his thing.

He rented a garage and found a job as a shoe salesman, his old occupation. Almost immediately he hit the road in his Ford and headed for Pennsylvania, his new territory. When, after a few months, he was still only breaking even, he insisted on trying a salaried job with an electrochemical engineering firm in the Bronx. After a week or so, Mutti made him quit. So he went back to being a shoe salesman, subscribing to the *Boot and Shoe Recorder*, and traveling to customers as far away as Washington, D.C., and Pittsburgh. He also joined Shimen in the First Naroler & Lipsker Benevolent Association to guarantee a family burial plot. Together with other Westerborkers, he became one of many Free Sons of Israel by joining Freedom Lodge #182.[3]

During the first few months following his arrival, we had been attending to our own affairs while Pappi filled the spaces we had kept open for him. Since 1942, when I turned fourteen and qualified for working papers, I had spent my summers working as a gopher in the stripping room of an offset printing company located on the East Side of midtown Manhattan. Manfred was working as a part-time soda jerk in the neighborhood. Thus, like

Mutti and Manfred, in July and August I was also out of the house. Fortunately, during the day Pappi did not have to be home alone with Mr. Krisinsky all the time, for Mutti would come home for four hours each day; if Mutti and I were both out, Manfred was often home. He learned to shop and cook those days when Mutti couldn't manage.

We made the most of Shabbes, for it was traditionally intended that the father play a dominant role on this family's day of rest. Almost immediately Pappi took charge and we were thrilled. Friday night changed dramatically. Whenever possible, Mutti arranged her four hours so that she could be with us to help with the preparations, light the candles, and hear Pappi sanctify the Sabbath with the kiddush, the same one our relative had proclaimed for all of us while we had filed past him in the deportation train to Zbaszyn. When Mutti had to return to her job, Manfred and I could have joined the other boys and cruised Sutter Avenue, but we didn't. On these summer evenings we strolled with Pappi and sometimes—when she could stay home—with Mutti. Oh, with what pride we did that!

Slowly Pappi became our Shabbes teacher, introducing us to his way of studying the Torah. It never occurred to either of us to ask him about his beliefs or reasons for observing some rituals and not others. We never inquired about how Westerbork had affected his faith in Judaism, and he almost never broached the subject. On one occasion he did tell me that most of the people he had known in the camp did not really undergo a change in character or religious beliefs during their camp experience. Applied to Pappi, that meant he was a modern, traditional, central European Jew whose religious practices were in harmony with ours in the neighborhood where we lived.

What a teacher he was! I had studied with many different Hebrew school teachers, but none of them ever drew me so deeply into one or two passages of text. Pappi knew so much about the sources and could read them in Hebrew or in Aramaic. Most important, he knew how to translate the commentators so that Manfred and I could both grasp the subtler meanings contained in these passages. After a while we were sitting for as long as two hours, not only deep in discussion but also feeling the joy and excitement of having Pappi fill the space we had left open for him.

As we withdrew Friday night from the domain of the profane, our home was transformed into a treasure I came to guard jealously during the first years of Pappi's return. As a high school senior and, later, as an evening student at Brooklyn College in 1947–48, I felt the peer pressure to spend Friday night differently. Before Pappi's arrival, we had not lived an Orthodox Jewish life. We were similar to most of the Jews in our neighborhood in that we were only partially observant—what an informed person at the time might have called functionally Conservative. Thus, all of us did many things on Shabbes that no self-respecting Orthodox Jew would ever do. It was hard to explain to friends and acquaintances why I insisted on staying home Friday nights.

"That's okay in high school, but not here in college. Come on, Korman. Grow up," was what the fraternity recruiter said while trying to sign me up at a midweek evening meeting. I had explained to him that my family worked all week and that we stayed at home Friday night to study. As he hammered me with a list of events that I would miss as a result of my Friday night absence, I realized I did not share any of his teenage rebelliousness against the older generation. So there was nothing to explain. He would never understand about that special space I had left for Pappi, the refrigerator at the Rifkins, the seder in Great Neck or in Talaton—those were the battlegrounds of my teenage rebellion. I told the recruiter: "If giving up my family Friday nights is the price of growing up, then I don't want to grow up."

In the next years those Friday nights became even more memorable when I discovered that Pappi was a marvelous guide for understanding my assigned readings in Milton. He had read him and appreciated the depth of his biblical knowledge. Pappi understood the Bible so well that as a junior, while enrolled in a course in English literature, I learned how to read Milton not in class at Brooklyn College but at father's table on Friday nights, shortly after we finished singing "Grace after Meals."

He also took up his reserved space in more personal ways. Except for wanting to be involved in my studies and listening to my reports of achievement or failure on the soccer field—neither he nor Mutti ever came to watch me play—Pappi hardly ever inquired into my affairs. He taught his lessons of acceptable social behavior by example, correctly assuming that Mutti had instructed us in matters of hygiene and personal conduct. He fretted about Manfred's bed-wetting and stutter. However, within a month after his arrival, in a dramatic homecoming event, Manfred stopped. Fortunately for all of us, there were no steady girlfriends to worry about. Sex education was reserved for the street crowd.

One conversation did touch on my general conduct. That exchange stunned me, for it went to the core of my teenage persona. For years I had parted my hair on the left side. By the time Pappi arrived, it had grown into a thick, wavy mop not unlike his own. As long as I cut it regularly, I thought it was pretty neat, as did my American friends. Mutti and Manfred had never suggested a change, nor had any barber, teacher, or girlfriend. Yet here was Pappi, a few months off the boat, suggesting that as a young man of eighteen I would look more mature if I combed my hair straight back, with no part on the side or in the middle, just straight back, the way he combed his. Without a word or a moment's hesitation I took a comb from my back pocket and re-styled my hair. I was thrilled. Pappi was home and suggesting how I might improve my looks.

Pappi's impact on the future of my education was profound. He had been in Westerbork when Mutti had urged me to try for Brooklyn Tech: "Refugees with trade skills always earned a living," she reminded me. "Go to the best technical school you can find and learn a trade. Then you'll be fine." So it never occurred to me that I should choose a college preparatory track designed to train potential engineers. I took courses to become an electrician. When Pappi realized what I was doing, he laughingly remarked: "A boy with two left hands training to become an electrician? It makes no sense." Of course, by then it was too late, for within months I expected to graduate.

The next two years, however, brought new choices. One of these sort of justified Mutti's approach: I worked in a small fluorescent-light assembly shop in Manhattan as a combination office and shipping clerk. The other choices reflected Pappi's preference. I enrolled in the evening session at Brooklyn College, expecting to take courses for many years in order to obtain a bachelor's degree with a major in history. Toward the end of the first year, Pappi insisted I stop wasting precious time. When I replied that as a family we could not afford to give up my twenty-eight dollars a week, he disagreed: "Parents and children grow as trees do. The little ones depend on the big ones for food and shade until they don't. Then the little ones must stand by themselves in order to become sturdy, mature trees. In time the big ones lean against the grown little ones. Your mother and I expect to work hard to support us. Now is the time for your independent growth. You must not sacrifice it. As a family we'll manage somehow," which we did. Although I switched to the day session, throughout my college days I continued to work after class, often thirty hours a week, not counting the subway rides in between.

From time to time Manfred and I thought about Yossel, but except for one brief encounter with some of his Brooklyn relatives or family friends, we heard nothing. Sadly, the connection had broken. Only much later did we learn about the dramas in his life after we abandoned him in 1940 when we left for the United States. That's precisely what we had done and that's how he felt about it—and he was right. Except for Paula and Freda, holdovers from that other world, he was now alone, abandoned by the two of us, whom he had come to love and trust. Of course, we had no choice but to go to our Mutti, as he would have gone to his had she reappeared. But the scar of abandonment remained on him and on us.

We had not been the only Jews to leave him alone. London's organized Jewry had also abandoned Yossel and the girls, not at once, the way we had to, but gradually, so that by 1943 the refugees from Otwock were all but forgotten by those who had vouched for them in 1939. Given the silence from Yossel's mother, the probability of a Christian claim increased. Then someone woke up. In response to complaints, the Christian executive director of the English Refugee Children's Movement was prompted to look at the Talaton children who "for some time have not received religious teaching, and have not been able to live an orthodox Jewish life."[4] Some Orthodox Jews were now alarmed that these youngsters—refugees and evacuees being reared in caring and loving Christian homes—would stop being Jewish. In fact, by 1946 it was public knowledge in England that Isa Scheider, whom I do not recall, and Paula and Freda had been baptized.

Not Yossel. In 1943 he was still in touch with his Jewish teacher and may well have assumed that his oldest sister had reached Palestine. After the Christian executive director of the Refugee Children's Movement had talked to him in Talaton, she reported: "He is very conscious of his Jewish birth and religion and most loyal, but he says his sister knows that their mother knows, through her, that he is living in a non-Jewish home and they do not want him moved."[5] How Joseph or the director—or, for that matter, how his sister—could have known what his mother thought about Yossel in Devon in 1943 boggles the mind. His older sister had managed to reach Palestine from a training farm in eastern Poland, but his mother and other sister were by then in wartime Soviet Russia. In any event, war-related catastrophes had intensified his mother's silence, so that at its conclusion Yossel came to be known in Talaton—and among his school friends of Ottery St. Mary—as Joe Kamiel, a kind of son in the Gosling household.[6]

Then the impossible happened. Yossel's itinerant Jewish teacher, who had stopped visiting sometime during the war, had found Yossel's mother and other sister. In 1945 he was part of an English group of visitors looking for Jewish survivors in the camps of the British Zone of Occupation. One day in Bergen-Belsen, while sitting around a table where some of the survivors shared their pictures of loved ones, Yossel's former teacher found himself staring at a photo of Yossel and at the pious Jewish woman, the Agudah mother whose picture it was. She was alive! She and her daughter, mother and sister, were sitting across from him. It seemed impossible, but here they were. After having let Yossel stay with the Kindertransport leaving Warsaw for England, mother and daughter were at first trapped by the German invasion. By November they had managed to cross into Russian-occupied Poland, where they made their way to Vilna. In June 1941 they again took flight from German invaders, traveling deep into eastern Russia, where they remained until the end of the war, at which point mother and daughter made their way back into the British Zone of Occupation and to Bergen-Belsen, which was now a DP camp.[7]

In time Yossel's mother hurried to London, but he had so bonded to the Goslings that he responded cautiously to his mother's overtures. Once a week he came visiting from Talaton, trying to relate to this ultra-Orthodox mother in London while desperately holding on to his sense of security in Christian Talaton and Ottery St. Mary. After a while he moved in with his mother, while still retaining his Gosling connections by visiting Rose Cottage once a week. It was a shattering experience, cutting short all sorts of plans and expectations, including a dream to attend university in nearby Exeter. So he resigned himself to his new life, became a bookkeeper, and for a long time remained alienated from the Jewish worlds of his mother and sisters.

There were also problems in our reunited family. Most of them were of a public nature—at least for me—because I was only beginning to sense and feel what Mutti and Pappi were keeping to themselves. No matter how hard they tried to keep the Westerbork experience out of our lives, too many complex emotions had been stirred for us to trust the healing process. When Westerbork friends came to visit, Mutti had no way of untangling innuendoes or comprehending a raised eyebrow or sly smile at the mention of names of women who were once and may still be important to her husband. It was hard for him to live with a woman who had inched her way to independence, who now walked as an upright New Yorker, with pride, dignity, and a sharp tongue. Perhaps I was overly protective because Mutti and I had so depended on each other during Pappi's absence, but I couldn't understand the way he second-guessed some of her decisions. Invariably he began to find fault with her within a minute after she arrived, often after she had just done last-minute shopping and was hastily preparing our food. He picked precisely that moment to voice a complaint, which I didn't like. She had only four hours each day to travel to and from her job, buy food and prepare meals, and do all sorts of other chores for us. Besides, I never did understand why Pappi didn't drive Mutti back to the subway station or bus stop. I didn't drive because it was self-evident that the car was Pappi's car; it was too risky to take it out on frivolous teenage joyrides. I also knew side-street parking was hard to find, and that Mutti loved to walk.

He never volunteered any information about Westerbork; for that matter, we hardly ever talked about Zbaszyn, the *St. Louis,* or the war in general. During his first few years in America, I can't recall ever asking him or his friends anything about camp life.

They rarely said anything and I was afraid to ask, afraid to find out in detail just how he and his friends had managed. (Among themselves, of course, when they were not preoccupied with the here and now of adjusting to life in New York City, they reminisced all the time about a world that they were convinced—and rightfully so—was beyond the comprehension of Mutti, Manfred, or myself.) For us it was enough to know that they had all escaped from the ash heaps of European Jewry, but I did start to become aware that we were all developing a sense of comparative physical and emotional suffering. Every once in a while—perhaps it had started at one of our first seders at home—Mutti felt compelled to remind Pappi's friends that as a Westerbork widow she had also suffered during the war. It sounded lame despite the fact we all understood that relatives and neighbors, like clerks in Jewish agencies, were defensive about their own problems and usually could not identify with any of our painful memories. They protected themselves through a distancing process, both then and in later years, by simultaneously helping refugees and complaining about them.

10

The first family seder in our sublet on Miller Avenue was, for various reasons, as complicated as the ones we had celebrated in Great Neck, Long Island. We did not have to make the kitchen kosher, but we did have to make it and the entire apartment fit for Passover. Besides the thorough cleaning, we needed to figure out how much of our kitchenware could be used. This time, of course, we could rely on Pappi, who was familiar with all the rules and—more important—understood the reasons behind them. It was in connection with this Pesach preparation that I really learned about the Talmudic concept of "fences" in the formulation of rules of ritual conduct. Pappi knew the differences between a fence and the essence of a principle that the fence was intended to protect. Such knowledge predisposed him to adopt a spirit of reasonableness when deciding what was permitted and what prohibited.

Since the first seder in 1947 occurred on a Friday night, the evening of April 4, almost all of our preparations had to be finished during the preceding work week. Compared to Nadnia or Talaton—or, for that matter, to Great Neck—Miller Avenue's seder preparations were easy. The stores in the neighborhood carried everything. Manfred and I knew that better than anyone since we had been Passover delivery boys in earlier years. We also had more money with which to buy dishes and pots to replace those that we needed but could not make kosher for Passover. And if, for some reason, we had to go out of the neighborhood for a special item, there was always Pappi's car.

This seder was definitely different! For one thing, we could invite guests. Since Pappi's arrival, we had visitors to the apartment and we would continue to have them after our two seders. (Once even Liesel Levy came, setting off all sorts of troubled feelings in Manfred and myself about this other woman who had been so important to Pappi during the year of liberation in Amsterdam.) This Pesach was also very special, which became apparent when we decided whom to invite. Some choices were obvious: Frank Aaron, now Frankie Weichman, whose new parents had decided to return to Germany and who had become a regular overnight Shabbes guest; Pappi's good friends from Westerbork—Erich, Vera, and Hilda Cohn and Betty and Walter Lenz—who, upon arriving in New York, all became part of our intimate social circle; and Mutti's cousin Wolf Engelberg, who had been so kind to us when his family was intact. In 1947 he was a divorced man and consequently liked to spend the Shabbes and holidays with our family, so we had him over as a guest whenever we could. Plus there were several others who came to those first seders on Miller Avenue.

Of course, before they arrived we had to prepare the kitchenware. Mutti used as many of her four hours each day to shop and clean, but it was Manfred who found the biggest metal pot and took it to the coal furnace in the basement. There he dunked and filled it with boiling water, placing the approved red-hot stone in it. Then he used the pot for dunking the silver wine cups, which my parents had somehow saved, and for all sorts of smaller pots and pans. He didn't have to do that for the drinking glasses because Mutti had been soaking those in the bathtub for three days. Manfred also didn't bother with the cutlery because Pappi had said he'd come home early enough to do that himself—he said he had a special method.

I arrived after Pappi had started. What a thrill it was to see him—dressed in slippers and wearing beltless, loose-fitting trousers—standing before the pot of boiling water and making the cutlery kosher for Pesach. His method consisted of tying each knife, fork, and spoon to a long string and, without touching them, systematically dunking our entire set of cutlery. I was impressed yet also realized there was something wrong. "Pappi, what's missing?" I asked, to which he replied: "Nothing, I think." "The stone! Where is the red-hot stone?" Stunned by the question, he stared at me and then burst into laughter, almost dropping the long cutlery string. "Stone? What stone?" I said:

"When we prepared the kitchenware, we always used a stone. You have to use a stone to make it all kosher for Pesach." With a knowing smile he asked: "Are you not a graduating senior from Brooklyn Technical High School?" After I nodded in agreement, he asked: "What's the boiling point of water?" to which I replied "212 degrees Fahrenheit." "So what's the problem?" he asked. "Isn't the water boiling on the gas stove the result of an even, continuous, and predictable source of heat? How much hotter would it get with a red-hot stone?" By now my flushed face reflected my embarrassment. "So where does the stone come from?" I inquired sheepishly. "Oh," he exclaimed, "in Narol we had no gas, so we had to use stones for reaching the highest possible temperature."

The seders themselves were also exciting. I had not remembered how Pappi conducted a seder. It was a new experience. We were in the care of a father comfortable with our family and confident about his capacities to lead it toward a better future. He was an experienced and knowledgeable discussion leader who, with a light touch, enveloped us with beliefs in God and discussions of Jewish Peoplehood. Some, like Frankie or the Cohns, were secular, but Pappi guided them toward tradition as a way of identifying themselves as Jews. Wolf was pious; he was delighted to be part of a larger group of Jews with whom he could identify. Many arcane questions and sophisticated commentaries alternated with observations on current events, especially about Jews still in Europe, events in Palestine, and about Palestinian politics in the United Nations, Washington, D.C., and London. We talked about past seders in Nadnia, Talaton, and Great Neck, but not once did we mention Westerbork. Silently the catastrophe bound us together, uniting Passovers past and future, perhaps in Jerusalem next year.

These days would become memorable for still another reason. A Passover incident making our refugee experiences a public event exposed the ways some influential American Jews interpreted our past seven years. When we started residing at the Petrovers, Manfred and I met some of their Horowitz relatives, "of Horowitz–Margareten, the matzo bakers, you know." However, this Horowitz was Eddie Horowitz, a distinguished pioneer and Hebrew-language educator in the city's public school system.

We spent a long lunch with him and told him all sorts of stories about our days in Poland and England. Six years later, when Manfred walked into his advanced Hebrew-language class at Thomas Jefferson High School, Eddie Horowitz introduced him to the class as the hero in one of the assigned stories Eddie had written in his Hebrew-language exercise book. Always a bit of a showman and entrepreneur, he called in photographers and reporters, who took photos while Manfred read Eddie's account of our Talaton seder.

The story of a refugee boy reading about himself in an assignment at Jefferson High was featured in the school's newspaper, the *Jeffersonian*, in some of the city's commercial papers, including the *New York Post*, the *New York Telegram*, and in the *Jewish Spectator*. There was a picture of Manfred standing among his seated classmates, reading from Eddie Horowitz's collection of Hebrew stories. He was a real hero who, at fifteen, had become one of the high school boys from the neighborhood, a handsome fellow with wavy black hair.

If not for the timing, the story would have ended there. In 1947 most Americans, including — perhaps especially — American Jews, did not want to hear yet another refugee tale. However, this particular Passover story had been published back in January, with enough time intervening to provide the lead time for the always alert American Jewish Committee (AJC) to consider it as the basis for a radio drama on its regular *Eternal Light* program broadcast on station WOR. Morton Wishengrad, a distinguished playwright who often wrote scripts for the program, arranged to meet with Manfred and Mutti. Thanks to them Wishengrad acquired enough details to render our Talaton seder in his radio play, which was called "The Bitter Herb." It was both exciting and troubling: although we couldn't figure out how to turn the contact into some desperately needed cash, we loved the publicity.

Except Pappi. He did what was necessary while keeping his distance from the entire affair. When we heard that Raymond Massey, then a famous actor of stage and screen, was going to narrate and play the role of Pappi and that, at the conclusion of the radio play, former governor Herbert H. Lehman was going to speak, Pappi did not share in our excitement. We were really going to be featured on the *Eternal Light* program! We told our friends to listen

8   THE COMMITTEE REPORTER, MAY, 1947

Welcome to America

Separated for years when they were uprooted by the Nazis, Mrs. Osias Korman and her sons were welcomed in New York by former Governor Herbert H. Lehman and Raymond Massey following a special broadcast presented by the American Jewish Committee over a nationwide hook-up. Governor Lehman called for emergency measures to admit "our fair share" of Nazi victims to the United States, while Mr. Massey was the narrator in "The Bitter Herb," a dramatization of the Korman family's experiences written by Morton Wishengrad. Left to right, Manfred Korman, Mr. Massey, Mrs. Korman, Governor Lehman and Gerhardt Korman.

AJC Staff Members Investigate Local Community Movements In Cooperation With National Planning Association Study

Dr. S. Andhil Fineberg, director of the American Jewish Committee's community service department, and Dean Manheimer, research associate in the scientific research department, are cooperating in a study of local community movements, conducted by the National Planning Association.

The study has been in progress since January, when the Association called a conference of the representatives of some 20 organizations. Dr. Fineberg attended for the AJC and Dr. Julius Schreiber represented the National Institute of Social Relations at the session where E. J. Coil, executive director of the National Planning Association, presided.

It was decided to call a national conference during the summer, to discuss types of community developments tending to unity and the cooperation of varied elements in the population. Organizations in the fields of business, labor, education, social welfare, church groups and others having community service or public relations departments, were asked to furnish investigators who would study community movements on the scene and prepare reports for the summer conference.

Dr. Fineberg headed a team which included staff members from the Federal Council of Churches of Christ in America, Colgate University, the New York Citizens Council and the Syracuse Planning Commission, who studied the Planning Council of Syracuse, N. Y., during the week of March 24. Mr. Manheimer worked with a team which conducted similar investigations in Schenectady, N. Y.

AJC JOINS CAMPAIGN AGAINST DISCRIMINATION IN BOWLING

The American Jewish Committee has joined with church, civic, labor and interracial organizations in combatting discriminatory practices against Negroes, Chinese, Hawaiians and Japanese in one of the country's most popular sports.

In a telegram to Olga Madar, recreation director of the United Automobile Workers, CIO, Dr. John Slawson, executive vice-president of the AJC, gave support to a Chicago conference called by the UAW-CIO to work out a plan of action to establish fair play in bowling competition. The American Bowling Congress, supreme authority in the sport, restricts league and tournament competition to the "white male sex."

Dr. Slawson's wire read: "The American Jewish Committee believes that discrimination in competitive sports because of race, color or creed is both un-American and unsportsmanlike and should be eliminated. We concur with any constructive efforts to eliminate discrimination in the national sport of bowling."

State Booklet Charts Intergroup Education

The progress of intercultural education in the schools of New York State is reported in a 100-page illustrated booklet published recently by the State Department of Education. Entitled "Education for Unity," the booklet outlines the activities being conducted in elementary and secondary schools and in adult education throughout the State. It has been distributed to administrators of public and private schools, teachers colleges and adult education groups and organizations.

To further intercultural education, the public school affairs committee of the AJC's New York chapter, in cooperation with a number of other organizations, has formed a joint committee which will formulate a program to meet the needs of New York City school children and will take steps to see that such a program is adopted by the City school authorities.

Represented in the joint committee, in addition to the chapter group, are the Anti-Defamation League of B'nai B'rith, the National Urban League, the National Conference of Christians and Jews, the Bureau for Intercultural Education, the Brooklyn Jewish Community Council, the United Parents Association and the Public Education Association. Delegate to the joint body from the chapter committee is Mrs. Carlos Israels.

Proskauer Letter Praises Heroism of Danish Monarch

Praise for the heroic stand of the late King Christian of Denmark against Nazi barbarism and anti-Semitism was expressed in a letter sent by Judge Joseph M. Proskauer, president of the American Jewish Committee, to the Danish minister in Washington, Henrik De Kauffmann, on April 21. Judge Proskauer's letter said, in part:

"With nothing less than heroism King Christian stood firm against Nazi efforts to debase Denmark's proud tradition of tolerance and equal opportunity for all irrespective of creed. And we know that in all ways possible, he sought to aid those suffering under the impositions of the Nazi barbarism.

"The shining sense of honor of King Christian was reflected in the conduct of the Danish people toward the Jews of their own and of neighboring countries. It is a solemn duty at this time for us to be mindful of this page of honor in Denmark's history and to record our gratitude and sense of obligation on the passing of your great sovereign."

Manfred, Raymond Massey, Mutti, Herbert H. Lehman, and author at the WOR radio station studios in Manhattan, 1947.

and looked forward to going to the studio, meeting the actors and the former governor, who was now the head of the United Nations' refugee relief organization! Not Pappi. He had decided to go to the Cohns and listen to the broadcast with them. There was no changing his mind.

So just the three of us went, with Mutti hoping there'd be a check at the end. We had heard about people attending radio broadcasts but had no idea what it was like. Every once in a while Mutti had taken Manfred and me to Radio City Music Hall because we had a relative among the Rockettes: Cilli Glücksmann's niece, Ruth Feldman, who had taken her first ballet lessons in Hamburg. But this invitation from the AJC to come to station WOR was obviously different. We dressed for the occasion, thinking that when we met the famous actors and politicians, we would feel properly attired in our new role as refugees on public display. For an instant, as we approached the doors to the studio in midtown Manhattan, I began to empathize with Pappi's decision, but once we were in the studio I was also pleased to be sitting with Manfred and Mutti among the rest of the small attentive audience. When the broadcast was over, while a flash photo was being taken someone introduced us as the Korman family. We said hello, shook hands with the cast, Raymond Massey, former governor Lehman, and left, but not before Manfred got the leads and the governor to sign his copy of the script. By the time we had returned to Miller Avenue, Pappi was already home.[1]

Part IV

The End of the Beginning

11

In retrospect, the radio play "The Bitter Herb" was part of the end of my decade-long emotional natal event. Together with hundreds of thousands of other Jewish refugees who had emigrated from Europe, I moved on with my family. We responded to the call from across centuries to find would-be cinders, to help turn them into blocks of their own choosing, to build with them and for them, and then, at each step of the way, to celebrate a birth, a Bar and Bat Mitzvah, a wedding, a circumcision.

My constructed past remained engaged: the nightmare, the shawl, and the nagging questions about a beloved father (What did Pappi do in Westerbork and how did he manage to do it?). That's why, without warning, a government official, a clerk at a Canadian border crossing or at a motor vehicle bureau, can trigger an anxiety attack even though I realize that each, at worst, can cause only an inconvenience. It was no different in 1947, when I ended my statelessness by becoming a U.S. citizen. I was so intimidated that I couldn't hear the official proclaiming the "Oath of Allegiance" until he declared, "So help me God." Fortunately, I had brought a college friend. "Ask him to repeat it," he whispered in my ear. I felt American, but that bold I was not. Nor, a few years later, could I directly answer a Canadian official who came through the railway car in the early dawn and demanded "Papers, papers, please" in that officious tone reserved for border-crossing guards the world over. I replied by pointing to the rack above me: "Just a minute. Just a minute. I am up there in my briefcase." "Where were you born?" he now demanded more sternly. "Elberfeld," I blurted out as I twisted my body so that my face could look at his while my left arm pulled down my briefcase, where I had packed my American citizenship papers. "Where is that," he barked. "Germany," I replied while handing him my precious document. He glanced at it, looked at me, and went about his business: "Papers, papers, please." I was exhausted.

When I see my belongings or those of loved ones, in sealed cartons or in suitcases, standing around, being packed or unpacked, or just waiting to be moved somewhere, I become quite apprehensive, as was the case in an Israeli absorption center, where I discovered, amid the boxes, that the difference between an immigrant and a refugee may only be a state of mind. Fresh-cut grass reminds me of the fields near Hamburg's Damthor railway station, where I used to play pick-up soccer and from where many deportations had occurred. When I see trains packed with human freight, whether actual or on television, I remember the transport into Zbaszyn and think of the many from Westerbork ending in a cinder sky. And I ask myself, which one of them could have been mine?

From the moment our family was again unified, the deportation days (in the secular calendar) and the seder days (in the Hebrew calendar) called forth formal moments of remembrance and reflection. These affected our collective recollections, which came to include experiences with the good people in Jewish public-service organizations. These individuals referred to refugees in the abstract and, later, as "displaced persons," the new euphemism for refugees and Jewish camp survivors.

For us "The Bitter Herb" represented a confrontation with fragments from our experiences selected by American strangers; it was their rendition of our yesterdays. They didn't understand Talaton and were quite indifferent to our everyday struggles and achievements on Miller Avenue. According to the script, we were religiously devoted Jews, tossed here and there by a storm beyond the saving hand of human intervention, the Talaton seder linking us to all those about to begin their annual encounter with the story of Exodus and Sinai. A small choir provided the liturgical themes, one obviously connecting the play to the Passover story and the other, by way of a well-known psalm fragment, to the ambiguities of human relations to God. The voices sang out, sometimes as sharp, piercing screams reflecting our abandonment, sometimes in angelic voices, as at the very end of the play, when Rosa intones "Blessed Be He Who Comes" for her arriving Osias, the miraculous resolution of our rescue and unification.

When Mutti managed to obtain recordings of "our" radio script, by listening to it we also participated in the transmission of the broadcast story. Eddie Horowitz, the reporters, the script-writer, and we Kormans had all done our part—differently, to be sure—but had done it nevertheless. Eddie had written a language exercise based on his recollections from a lunch with two little boys in 1940. He garbled the story and shaped it to suit his purpose, namely, as a language-instruction exercise for reinforcing Jewish values he held dear. The reporters who came to Jefferson structured their accounts around this tale and the classroom event that dramatized Eddie's noble passion: the teaching of modern Hebrew in a New York City public school.

Morton Wishengrad used the tale for his good Jewish causes, especially for mobilizing public opinion to help get Jewish DPs out of Europe. He knew little more about us than did Eddie and worked just as hard to keep it that way. But he was well informed about contemporary Jewish problems. As the AJC cosponsored the *Eternal Light* series with station WOR, the play had to stress noncontroversial themes. The AJC was a secular watchdog and lobbying organization on behalf of domestic and international Jewry; in 1947 it was still not supporting the campaign for the establishment of a Jewish state in Palestine. Under the pressure of postwar Jewish requirements in Europe and Palestine, however, the AJC was eager to cooperate with Zionists on issues or programs where their interests overlapped. The AJC could sponsor or associate itself with a religiously oriented radio drama that did not directly and explicitly raise subjects that it perceived as controversial or embarrassing to Jews in the United States. Thus, in his script Wishengrad made brief, symbolic, yet powerful allusions to the fact that the United States had also refused to accept the passengers of the *St. Louis*, to six million Jewish dead in Europe, and to the British internment on Cyprus of thousands of Jews trying to get into Palestine. Nevertheless, the play never strayed from its noncontroversial orientation.[1] (It did not do so even in the epilogue of the broadcast, when former governor Lehman, the onetime political voice of New York Jews in the

Democratic Party but now speaking on behalf of United Nations Relief and Rehabilitation Administration [UNNRA], made a nonsectarian appeal for all DPs in Europe.)

We Kormans also used our experience to meet certain needs and opportunities as best we could. We did, after all, participate in the making of "The Bitter Herb." When Manfred relayed a few detailed questions, Pappi answered them, read and corrected a draft of the script when it was sent home, and together with Mutti signed the required release forms. Before that I had written about my experiences in classroom exercises, adapting the story to glory in the patriotic zeal of wartime America.

There was a difference in the way each of us did our part. In those years I did not think about the murder of European Jews in terms of political theology, or of my role in transforming a private and public catastrophe into a private and public memory. True, in 1946, over a cup of coffee in that shop in the old Metropolitan Opera building, I had once asked Artie Levine how we could rear children in a period that had produced Auschwitz and Hiroshima. However, I was proceeding cautiously.

I knew my American English was closer to the language the guys on Miller Avenue spoke, which was different from the sounds my parents and their immigrant friends made, and different, too, from those of my New World Club fellow soccer players, who were just a few years older, that is, old enough to have made German their language before leaving Europe; theirs was the German-accented English New Yorkers associated with Washington Heights! Mine was a variant of East New York English, which speech courses in Brooklyn College tried to mold into what instructors called "General American," the only version they considered fit to teach New York City's dialect-ridden public school children. Of course, when strangers asked, as they were wont to do in those years, "What's your nationality," and I replied, "American," they knew better: "Yea. O.K. But what's your nationality?" And they were right, because they actually meant ethnicity; no matter what "nationality" the stranger belonged to, the question almost always also sounded like an accusation: "Jewish, right? Not quite American, like us."

I took my first steps on Jewish New York's sidewalks, its playing fields, classrooms, and workshops, where my and their

"American" and "nationality" collided and intermingled in usually friendly ways. Public subways, bus and telephone lines, streets, parks, city buildings and their officials enveloped us all, imposing the same routines, shapes, and sounds we had come to expect. However, no matter where we lived and worked, the city also allowed us new immigrant Jews to preserve our special informal networks of relatives and friends, who almost always had shared part of the Nazi experience. Upon graduation from high school, I knew I had to earn money on a full-time basis. So when Mr. Schaefer, the old family friend who had unsuccessfully tried to get Pappi from the *St. Louis* to England, offered me a job in his fluorescent-lamp assembly shop, working for him and Gary, his black technical expert, I accepted and tried my best to hold on to it. By then I had also decided to become a history teacher. Brooklyn College's evening program was convenient: by subway it was only a forty-five-minute ride, from East Twenty-third Street, where I worked, and forty-five minutes to Van Sicklen on the New Lots line. Except for a small registration fee, each semester was free!

I was taking one step at a time, with some awareness of a larger view but without a strong sense of empowerment to shape the steps or choose the path. When I switched to the day session, I majored in history and minored in education to qualify as a certified teacher in New York City's high schools. The program demanded a whole range of required courses, including a speech class. I also joined the soccer team, although that decision proved not too smart, considering my thirty-hour workload with Mr. Schaefer. Yet it was the right thing to do: I loved soccer and knew that a lot of the other players had also been refugees.

I was gradually becoming a self-centered, family-oriented immigrant teenager. In 1948 I was thrilled that we Jews finally had our own state, a dream fulfilled without me being there. That was it: I cut my losses and went on to whatever was left, leaving an emotional memory available for instant revitalization. I did not become involved in organized Jewish life on campus, nor, for that matter, in any Jewish youth groups except, of course, for the New World Club. One summer I did spend a week at the camp of the International Zionist Federation of America, but I did that for the fellowship of a couple of friends from Brooklyn College who thought we would meet some nice girls there.

Brooklyn College friend Alex Blumberg and author, 1950–51.

As an immigrant family, we were all moving within that larger America about which we had learned a lot. In the city Pappi was now our scout and commander. With his Ford he traveled throughout the different boroughs, where he saw all sorts of neighborhoods and apartments for rent. During his first days on

Manfred, Pappi, Mutti, and author in Astoria, Queens, 1948–49.

Miller Avenue, he must have decided to get out of Mutti's tenement-house arrangements with old man Krisinsky, to get us out of the Miller Avenue apartment as soon as possible and into a neighborhood with new apartments and scenic views. In December 1948 he moved us near the East River, to Astoria, a part of Queens where gas storage tanks, the stately old railway bridge of the New Haven line, and the grand sweep of the then new Triborough Bridge shaped the horizon. It was here that he had brought us to make the real new start after liberation.

Marine Terrace was a private housing development whose tenants were of mixed ethnic backgrounds. We rented a two-bedroom apartment on the ground floor at ninety-three dollars a month, which was no more expensive than the rent plus Krisinsky's maintenance costs on Miller Avenue. There were no ceiling leaks, so there was no need for a bucket whenever it rained hard. Everything about the place looked and felt clean. It was all ours, including the spills and odors. It was also small. In the kitchen the stove stood so close to the window that one day a gust of wind ignited the curtains; I yelled and Manfred rushed in and tossed them into the sink. There was a dining area and a separate living room where a Shabbes guest could sleep on the sofa. Frankie Weichman came often, traveling all the way from his rooms near Brooklyn College.

The room where Manfred and I slept and worked was really meant for one person. Our narrow double bed filled the entire floor space, except for the few inches allotted to a pinewood folding table. It stood in the doorway, with both flaps down when we did not have to write on it; when we did, one of us sat on the bed while the other sat on a chair and lifted the opposite flap.

Except for Pappi, whose car made Astoria as convenient as Miller Avenue had been, we had to learn new travel routes to and from work and school. Mutti's job as a baby nurse took her all over the city. She now had to first take a bus to catch the subway into Manhattan or Brooklyn. Manfred, who had one semester remaining before graduating from Thomas Jefferson High School, had to make a radical change; instead of walking to school, he had to ride one hour on buses and subways, via Times Square, to get to his classes on time. Later, when he attended Queens College, the routes changed but the commuting distance remained more less the same. My round-trip commute time doubled, whether I was going to Brooklyn College or my job in Manhattan.

It was all new and different, preparing us for the future moves that would transport us far from where we had been. In the next few years Manfred and I left the city to pursue careers in education and raise families of our own. Mutti and Pappi moved, too, although they stayed in Queens. In 1953 Pappi found another new apartment in Briarwood, within walking distance of a synagogue and the nearby shops of Queens Boulevard and its stop on the F train. Minutes from the tall Scandinavian Airlines building and the borough's great highway complex, the apartment would also provide easy connections to the rest of Long Island to the east and the rest of America to the north, south, and west.

From Briarwood Mutti and Pappi made their pilgrimages. Mutti traveled to Talaton to see Miss Gosling and envelop her in an embrace of deep gratitude. Although she found her in good health, the once vibrant Ruth Gosling had turned into a hermit. Her mother had died and Yossel was now living in London. Even though Ruth hardly ever left her cottage, Mutti persuaded her to go to the seashore near Sidmouth. Pappi never returned to Europe, but around the time Mutti went to Talaton he visited Israel—a Zionist dream fulfilled—to see his sister, Resi, and his friend Liesel and her children.

The author at Manfred's wedding in Manhattan, 1954.

Mutti and Pappi at Manfred's wedding, 1954.

It was in that Briarwood apartment, where Manfred and I often stayed for extended periods, that our parents heard about girlfriends and many other trials and tribulations on the road to becoming—in the case of Manfred—a soldier, math teacher, and principal, and myself—an American historian who turned into an early student of the Holocaust. There Mutti and Pappi first entertained Mona Widder from Rego Park, Queens, whom Manny married during his military service in Colorado, and Ruth Zloten from Winnipeg, whom I married while we were both graduate students at the University of Wisconsin. Starting in 1956, it was in that selfsame apartment that my parents played with the first of six grandchildren. It was also there, in Briarwood, that we would mourn on occasion, rescuing memories from among remains tucked away in filing cabinets, drawers, and bookcases.

Epilogue

"You have to meet these people. They are from Amsterdam. I met them on the bus coming home. We are going to have coffee with them tonight, at their hotel in Jerusalem." Then Ruth went into the kitchen to prepare supper. "Who," I asked. "The Mouweses. He comes from a very old Dutch Jewish family dating back to 1648. It's the way he talked about the war. I don't know why. You have to meet them." It was 1984, fourteen years before the unveiling of Oswald's plaque in Wuppertal, a year after Mutti's death, and some twenty years since she had given me Pappi's Westerbork papers, which contained letters from Etty Hillesum.

During our conversation in the hotel lobby, where Joop and Bets Mouwes shared some of his searing wartime stories, it occurred to me that he might know Etty. "Of course. Of course. In Holland today everyone has heard of her. Her diary was published. It's been translated. A front-page review in the *New York Times Book Review*. How come you don't know?" I was initially stunned and then told him of my connection. "When we get back home tomorrow," Joop said, "I shall be your messenger to Mr. Gaarlandt," the Amsterdam publisher of the diary. Three days later an excited Jan G. Gaarlandt was on the phone telling me that he would visit me in Jerusalem to discuss the publication of those of Etty's letters I owned.

The next few weeks demonstrated what every professionally trained historian knows but does not always examine and write about: the impact of personal experiences on scholarly striving to understand the past. On this occasion there were multiple considerations: How many of the letters should I show him? How could I safeguard Pappi's reputation from exploitation? Did I have a right to sell them from an ethical standpoint? Stated differently, who really "owned" the letters, the recipient and his descendants or the writer and her descendants? More practically, there was the question of who should publish them and in which library they should be stored. On and on the questions multiplied. In hindsight, I increasingly felt compelled to examine a related but to me quite important issue: What was the impact of those ten years after 1938 on my formal study of the Holocaust. As a student of American history, I asked myself how they fit into the larger schemes of things, which I had been trying to understand for a long time.

There were internal professional influences that helped to explain the persistent striving to have my own voice heard regarding the conceptual need to comprehend the Holocaust as a historical phenomenon. Some of these had become self-evident by 1971. I was scheduled to read a paper at the first panel discussion of the American Historical Association (AHA) devoted to the Holocaust. Other influences became clear only much later when, at the invitation of historian Steven Zipperstein, I wrote a paper for delivery at Stanford University's Jewish Studies Seminar; the experience forced me to probe more deeply.

In 1971 I had accepted an invitation from Dr. Hannah Arendt to come to her Manhattan apartment to discuss my paper. She had decided not to critique the panel's papers but did want to talk to me about mine, which she liked. For me the importance of the conversation did not derive from her compliment, for which, of course, I was grateful. She provided an opportunity for discussing Euro-American frameworks of political economy and nationalism within which I perceived two documents that had long haunted my historical imagination. The first was a mid-eighteenth-century bill of sale from the New England slave trade. The second was a Nazi cost-accounting statement itemizing profits from incinerating bodies.

I described my reaction when, as a graduate student, I first read the bill of sale. Imagine a hired sea captain making all those entries: in the columns on the left he listed nails, shingles, a few girls and boys, some men and women, and kegs of rum; toward the right side of the page there was a price, multiplied for each item of cargo. Finally, in the last column on the right the captain expressed everything in terms of the cash nexus of commercial capitalism: He drew a line beneath all those numbers, allowing humanity to disappear so completely that among other expenses he could subtract a port tax, draw another line—the bottom line—to arrive at a grand total of money earned, valuable numbers made fit for New England's market disposition.

The Nazi document, which I had seen for the first time a few years later, was quite different, yet for me it also reflected the established commercial expression of a civilization where bookkeepers and accountants transvalued and reified all sorts of abstractions. After all, starting in the 1850s, railroad companies in the American republic had calculated profits on the basis of unit cost, cargo, or passengers per mile of track. When linked to long cattle drives and slaughterhouses, those tracks—and the people who owned and administered them—became part of a commercial processing system that transported mooing cows to human dinner tables and Native Americans into Russian pale-like reservations, holding pens for possible extinction.

Now, in the midst of World War II, a trained Nazi accountant calculated in reichsmarks "estimated profits obtained from hiring out [a Jewish inmate] . . . less food . . . less amortization for clothes . . . [for an] average life expectancy [of] 9 months x RM 5.30 [a day, plus] income from an efficient utilization of corpses (1) gold from teeth (2) clothes (3) valuables (4) money . . . less cost of burning (the corpses) . . . [resulting in an] average net profit [of] RM 2.00"; or, written just below the bottom line, beneath the columns of figures of reichsmarks, "1,631, to which must be added income from utilization of the bones and ashes."[1] Surely, I told Dr. Arendt, these quite disparate documents, spanning two hundred years of American and European history, reflect much more than stages of capitalism or manifestations of economic history. In play, in their own time and place, were race, ethnicity, religion, biocultural determinism, and the politics of governing regimes, the very stuff of particular—and particularly horrendous—ancient and modern tribal fires.

It required a challenging mingling of personal and professional experiences in order for me to be able to formulate these insights. But in time, in my studies of the history of America's forced and free migrations, I had come to appreciate the delicate membranes separating primitive and civilized, tribal and modern. Then it was obvious. I had to confront the phenomenon of the Holocaust as an American historian; for, speaking as an amateur poet,

Lines from a hand of human kin

bottom lines
quill-pen thin
or with a fountain pen

can cross a moral abyss of unfathomed dimensions.

Slavery and I engaged early and late, first triggered in those ten years but developed only gradually thanks to my American professional training. Early, because I first heard about it in the spring of 1939 in that *St. Louis* letter from my father, read when we were still in Zbaszyn. In it he had compared Jews of his time unfavorably to African slaves of the past: no one wanted to buy Jews. Late, because it was not until after Word War II, during my student days at Brooklyn College, that I learned how to read about the African American experience. Some of my classmates had organized a protest against the parochial or bigoted approach of historians who had written about slavery in the United States. One of the displayed books was by Arthur C. Cole, a star of the Department of History and one of the most knowledgeable historians of the antebellum American South and its slaveholders. He was upset not because he was opposed to a new look at America's "Peculiar Institution" but because the students had not done justice to the texts they were attacking. He could not tell whether his book had been chosen to illustrate the "right" or "wrong" approach to the subject. But he did know that if the critics had turned the page, they would have found an important qualification of passages on the previous page.

In the 1950s this exercise in critical distancing was reinforced during my graduate schooling in Madison, Wisconsin. I applied it to an important lesson my father had taught me about reading works by general secular historians touching on Jewish history. Pappi's lesson was accompanied by a *New York Times* article by Arnold Toynbee, who in some Jewish circles gained special notoriety when he designated postbiblical Jewry a fossil. After reading Toynbee, my father warned me of the "Hazer Fiessel," that is,

Pappi and author, just north of New York City, 1951–53.

"the pig's foot," the presence of an anti-Jewish subtext in the work of such a great English scholar and stylist. Was my father's "anti-Jewish" too strong a term? Perhaps not, if Toynbee's intent in that article was also to place Jews, Jewry, and Judaism on a staircase leading nowhere.

In Madison I came to realize that the seemingly objective language of my teachers and that of my anticlerical and anti- or non-Zionist Jewish classmates could also contain that subtext, not unlike what a devious kosher butcher might do when trying to pass off pork for kosher meat: see, the split hoof; not a word about chewing the cud.

In the governing frames of reference—some would later call them "regimes"—of teacher as well as of critical classmate, white immigrant groups—and stiff-necked Jewry in particular—were fundamentally of transitory importance in American life: In the long sweep of history, these collectives were fated to become part of the working class, or part of the large lower and middle class somehow being shaped by American market-fueled segregated melting pots. Comfortable in their constructed political economies, Wisconsin teachers and classmates seemed not to have appreciated the presence of multiple group loyalties of the kind that I felt in myself and that I was finding in my studies of German Americans in Wisconsin before World War I. Within American civic devotions and national passions, we had identities of our own, loyalties that comfortably lived side by side with other kinds, like membership in political parties, devotion to Lutheranism or Catholicism (in the case of German Americans), or to a class-oriented social democracy favored by some of the voters who supported Victor Berger's Milwaukee brand of socialism. These American identities and loyalties were as permanent or temporary as any of those to which teachers and classmates granted exclusive American permanence.

By 1957, when I began publishing on this subject, I was beginning to find my own voice, perhaps because I was no longer a single graduate student exclusively devoted to Clio, the Greek muse of history. My first year in Madison, Wisconsin, had been quite different from that of my Jewish New York. My Madison had a Jewish neighborhood, but it was more mental, associated with synagogues, Bnai Brith Hillel, and a kosher butcher shop. It was different because for me Madison was more like Talaton. This time I was entirely alone, green as grass—without even my own typewriter—among gifted fellow graduate students and professors.

Studying was my life, my comings and goings responding to class schedules and assignments, especially seminar assignments. My world was circumscribed by the location of university libraries, the student union, classroom and office buildings, nearby cafes and cafeterias, and neighborhood stores and laundromats. That is to say, I did not go out of my way to visit Jewish institutions or agencies—that stuff was all in my head. Ritual observance I left to others.

Except, of course, on the High Holy Days. Right from the start I realized that my mental baggage distinguished me from some of the other Jewish graduate students in my seminar. When they heard that I had told our professor that I would not be attending his seminar because of a Jewish religious holiday, they thought I was out of my mind: "It's not done in graduate school," they warned. "You'll pay for it."

That was 1951–52. In the next few years, the Holocaust—not yet so named—notwithstanding, prewar kinds of antisemitism still manifested themselves, which did not surprise most of the Jews who arrived in Madison from metropolitan New York, or, for that matter, Jews who had been longtime residents of Milwaukee, like some of Mutti's relatives. I took the presence of antisemitism for granted among fellow students and teachers, although I was always prepared to find my "Goslings," of which there were a few among professors and friends. However, when I asked to be excused from that first research seminar, I had not taken the measure of Howard K. Beale, the mentor who was to make possible my academic career in American history.

Pay for it? He took quite seriously his white civil rights devotions and his take on Presbyterianism. Indeed, for him religion established a special bond between us, if only because in his seminar I was the only student with an active public Jewish commitment. He was a patrician whose conduct often manifested attitudes some of us—who were perceived as escapees from the unwashed New York masses—viewed as patronizing, even as we sensed and sometimes heard the presence of the genteel antisemitism then commonly associated with academic life.

In time I found my friends—even a girlfriend from rural Wisconsin, whose family background reflected a mixture of religious beliefs and nationalities—students who wore the badge of

Attorney Gino Giugni (originally from Genoa, Italy), a dear friend from grad-uate school, and author, 1952–53.

Graduate student friends Ed Richards, correspondent Danilo Granchi (from Rome, Italy), the author, and Ping Chiu (from Beijing, China) in Vilas Park, Madison, 1952–54.

academic neutrality toward attitudes that all too often drove so many of our relatives and fellow citizens to commit acts of bigotry. I felt that we, the small collective, were different, comparable in spirit to the enthusiastic credo of neutrality a Jewish university student naively thought reigned in his mid-nineteenth-century Russian university, where, in fact, neutrality was invariably clothed in the deceptive universalistic language of Saint Paul in his letter to the Galatians: Jews and Gentiles together, all within the spirit of Jesus Christ.

I was not that naive about our larger university world, but during one Christmas a classmate did surprise me. It was mid-afternoon in the Wisconsin State Historical Society, where most of us graduate students in American history usually did our research. Upon leaving, I spotted a fellow student, went over to him, stretched out my hand, and wished him a merry Christmas. He took my hand and smiled. I turned to go, but as I walked toward the exit I heard him say: "And a Happy Easter to you, too. At least you had something to do with that." I heard the intended cut, recovered, wheeled round, and headed right back. "I am sorry, I didn't hear you," I said. Blushing until his face turned red, he nevertheless remained adamant: "A Happy Easter to you, too. At least . . ." I cut him off. "That's what I thought you said. Merry Christmas."

That experience I could share only with one of my friends. George Rawick had a similar encounter while grading history papers in Bascom Hall in a room set aside for teaching assistants. Across from his desk two other assistants were discussing Jews. Silently George looked up and stared. They joined in his silence and then, embarrassed, said something like "You're not . . ." "Aha," he replied, and returned to work. When he told me the story, he also said: "To them I looked Irish."

During my "first" Madison, the Jewish bond with George was quite special. He was brilliant and intellectually generous to a fault. Like others in Madison at the time, I learned much from him, particularly about his democratic socialism and his Marxist reading of American history. But he and I also discussed Jewish subjects, if only because he enjoyed telling me about his Jewish neighborhood in Brooklyn's Crown Heights, where his grandfather, an Orthodox rabbi, loved to take the sun on his favorite bench on Eastern Parkway. George and I also shared religious

George Rawick, a close friend from graduate school, in a photograph taken many years later when he was a distinguished professor of history at the University of St. Louis.

events. One Yom Kippur became memorable because we violated fundamental rules in our tradition. It began uneventfully. As the sun sank, we rushed from the campus to our respective rooms, changed, met in front of my rooming house, and walked quickly to the Conservative synagogue. There, in the crowded sanctuary, we participated in evening prayers and listened to the rabbi's sermon. When he started to preach about Joe DiMaggio and Marilyn Monroe, I felt compelled to walk out. Feigning a coughing fit, I hurried down the center aisle to the vestibule, where, after a few minutes, George joined me; he, too, had been offended. Then, in an act of rebellion, we decided to dine at one of our favorite Italian restaurants. By candlelight we discussed what we had just done on this Yom Kippur—for me, euphemistically, my one and only Protestant Yom Kippur. Without so much as mentioning the rest of the twenty-four-hour fast, the following

Ruth Zloten, University of Wisconsin genetics graduate student, in laboratory office in the Department of Veterinary Science, 1955–56. We were married in 1956.

morning, as I left my rooming house ready to return to shul, there was George waiting for me.

My "second" Madison started in 1955, when Ruth Zloten, Jewish to her fingertips, entered my life. With "Peoplehood" battle flags flying, she welcomed me to her castle. In no time at all I reconnected with the entire Jewish calendar, and not just Pass-over, the High Holy Days, and Hanukkah. As a married couple, we moved our Jewish castle wherever we went: first into Madison and later into small towns in upstate New York, to Elmira and then to Ithaca, some thirty miles to the north, at the southern edge of Lake Cayuga. Imperceptibly our lifestyle also permeated my work as a professional historian.

During that first year of marriage she related a dramatic story not unlike those told in my father's circle. Ever the hard-working graduate student in microbial genetics, she had just returned from her laboratory. It was Christmas Eve. A postdoctoral fellow from Italy was also working late that afternoon. In the course of the regular chit-chat among lab colleagues, she asked him: "How do you celebrate Christmas?" He replied: "Oh! In Italy families gather the way they do here. Many go to church; but many don't." He went on to describe what the streets looked like. When Ruth asked: "But how does your family celebrate Christmas," he responded by relating some details about his wife and children. Finally Ruth realized that she had to ask him one more question: "And you, who are here in the laboratory, how do you celebrate Christmas?" To which he gave the following response: "Me? You don't know? With my last name you, of all people, don't know. Segre! Segre! The famous Spanish river near the French border. Segre! The river Jews crossed when they ran away from the Spanish Inquisition. I am Jewish, Ruth, like you. After they fled, my ancestors took the name Segre. But my parents considered themselves Italian anti-vivisectionists, which meant many things, but it also meant they were opposed to circumcision. Despite all that, with our name and lineage, the Germans murdered my mother in Auschwitz."

In 1965–66, when I first began to teach and write about the Holo-caust, the subject of the Jewish catastrophe in World War II already had a significant corpus and particularizing language reaching back to 1940. Thanks in large part to the efforts of dedi-cated scholars and administrators devoted to contemporary Jew-ish history—including Jacob Robinson, Philip Friedman, Jacob Lestschinky, Max Weinreich, and Isaiah Trunk—this body of work was supported by institutes and boasted an ongoing multi-volume, multilingual bibliographical project that encompassed publications from Yiddish-language printing houses in Mexico, Argentina, and Tel Aviv, as well as other books and articles written in the main languages spoken by Jews in Europe, the United States, and Israel.

Among my fellow U.S.-based academic historians working outside the field of Jewish history, an entirely different intellectual regime existed. By then I had gained some perspective on my graduate training, which had not even broached this subject, and had come to better appreciate the American historiographical framework within which the Jewish catastrophe would have to find its place. In 1962 David Potter, a master historian, had called upon his colleagues to stop writing about nationalism and nationality as if both were unchanging and monolithic. Instead, he had urged them to write about the subjects on the basis of what they, in fact, knew to have taken place in the lives they studied. During the next few years, when what later came to be known as identity politics all but swamped urban media and academic rhetoric, I came to understand how perceptions of the Holocaust on my terms would be buffeted by perceptions of African American and immigrant group life within America's nationalism. Established American historians, who had constructed Anglo-Americans and their dynamic class formations, usually had not treated those groups as also constituting complex legitimate American ethnic collectives, with pasts and transcontinental mental connections of their own. For such Americanists the Holocaust conceptually represented an especially nasty anti-Jewish German war atrocity, a variant of one of many experienced by Europeans during World War II: To them this was another human act of mass murder; or, as George Kennan stated in 1943, was part of the "customs of warfare" one had come to expect in wars on the eastern front involving our ally, Soviet Russia.[2] Indeed, like every other atrocity committed by Europeans, this one was understood as being outside America's history and therefore not part of mid-twentieth-century professional American historical writing.

These historians placed events of the Holocaust beside events ostensibly not affected by U.S. policies, such as the pogroms in Russia and Poland, European antisemitism in the decades preceding World War I, and the mass killings and ethnic cleansings of the interwar years. My teachers and colleagues in American history would not or perhaps could not—indeed, it took me a while—recognize this particular catastrophe of World War II as part of a Euro-American history, one haunted by deadly forced migrations across the middle passage of the Atlantic and the lands of the western plains. Nor could such historians typically comprehend the Holocaust in another context. Before World War I, European attitudes, practices, and policies were influenced by America's magnetic impact on steam-powered migration movements within the great empires of central Europe. After World War I, U.S. commercial tariff barriers, restrictive immigration policies, and a fascination with eugenics all affected European economic policies and biocultural politics in complex ways.

For students of modern history, what had come to be designated the Holocaust in the late 1950s did not exist, neither in textbooks or academic monographs purporting to cover the twentieth century in Europe and America, nor in articles and book reviews in scholarly journals. As I was later to learn, in the publications of a few Jews the Holocaust served as a powerful influence—not always obvious yet constantly at work. One master historian I especially admired personally and professionally was George L. Mosse, whose studies proved invaluable in my own engagement with this subject. I thought I had understood his deeper concerns from the start, but I was never certain, not until I read his book *Confronting History*, which was published posthumously. At the very end of his life he publicly acknowledged the constant presence of the Holocaust in his work as a professional historian. On the last page of his final chapter, entitled "The Past as Present," he wrote: "My acceptance of myself was set within the constant awareness of a past which refused to go away, and indeed I did not try to transform or overcome the vivid feeling that I was a survivor. The Holocaust was never far from my mind; I could easily have perished with my fellow Jews. I suppose that I am a member of the Holocaust generation and have constantly tried to understand an event too monstrous to contemplate."[3]

I met George Mosse when he first came to Madison as a most special person: he was the first Jew to be given a tenured appointment by "my" all-white male Department of History. At the time I was deeply immersed in a dissertation on American

modernization—about Milwaukee's industrialization, urbaniza-
tion, immigration, and reform—and did not have the good sense
to audit his lectures in European history. I started reading his
works a few years later, when I was teaching a course on Western
civilization to first-year students at Elmira College. There I had
met the late George Kren, a fellow refugee from Vienna, who was
one of Mosse's first graduate students. He suggested I read his
professor's book on German volkish thought.

In the ensuing years it was not so much the power of that
scholarship as the unusually charged public American debate
about Jewish conduct during the Nazi period that pushed me.
The crossover passions deriving from the struggle for civil rights
and early protests against America's involvement in Vietnam
made me realize that although the Holocaust was being invoked
indirectly in rhetoric and symbolism, as a phenomenon it was not
being acknowledged by colleagues in my profession; the Nazi
campaign against all Jews in lands occupied by the German army
hardly ever received any special attention at all. Though not the
first, as American professional Europeanists Raul Hilberg, in his
monumental *Destruction of European Jewry,* and Arendt, in her
controversial *Eichmann in Jerusalem,* had each faced the subject
head-on in works that in time became especially well known.
Neither was a working professional historian, nor, for that matter, did either conceive of the Holocaust as a historical phenomenon at the time. Their frames of reference were different: for Hilberg the political scientist it was bureaucracy in the German
Third Reich; for Arendt the comparative political theorist it was
totalitarianism in a modern nation-state. Indeed, at the time it
seemed to me that their generalizations in these books about Jewish conduct during the catastrophe rested less on direct evidence
and Jewish scholarship than on erroneous or exaggerated stereotypes about Jewish conduct in the Diaspora.

I was also perplexed and disturbed by the work of a handful
of American historians who used the catastrophe to acquire a
deeper understanding of African American conduct during the
time of enslavement. Instead of turning to the available professional multilingual Jewish scholarship, Stanley Elkins and his
first group of critics relied on Bruno Bettelheim, Eli Cohen,
Eugen Kogon, and Arendt, that is, on contemporaries and their

controversial and limited observations and insights about Jewish conduct in Nazi camps. Dehumanization, anomie, agency, and resistance leaped out of the texts, but without the contexts historians require for describing and analyzing events and catastrophes involving millions of differentiated peoples living and dying in vast and variegated territories. How could they do that? In studying American slavery, these same important authorities employed the corpus of their profession's scholarship in their critical evaluations of eyewitness accounts and insights dating from antebellum days.[4]

In other words, in 1965–66 I was not upset over the comparative frame of reference. I was gaining insights for comprehending the Holocaust from professional historians of American slavery: a year or two later at Cornell University, it was a lecture by C. Vann Woodward on the moments of liberation at the end of the Civil War that taught me to appreciate and conceptualize the moments of liberation at the end of World II. (For that reason there is a section in my book *Hunter and Hunted* entitled "Liberation.") I was appalled at the American provincialism, ignorance, and presumptuousness that governed the approach and use of recent Jewish experience in circumstances about which so much was still to be learned. To my mind, the historians' conduct was almost as outrageous as Betty Friedan's use in *The Feminine Mystique* of Jews in concentration camps to dramatize the place of suburban housewives in American society.

It was in this mood that I began to teach a course on the Holocaust. A few years before I presented a paper at the AHA conference in New York, I wrote two papers that flowed directly from my new teaching efforts. The first was not a paper at all but rather a long letter to Hillel Rabbi Max Ticktin, an old friend from my graduate student days in Madison, who was then assigned to the Washington, D.C., office of his organization. I sent him a report of what I had undertaken during an informal Hillel seminar at Cornell: a discussion of Euro-American xenophobia during the interwar years; an examination of immigration restrictions; a detailed explanation of how I used the movements of the German army as an engine of change; a discussion of Jewish life in selected cities before their occupation; and, finally, an analysis of the Jews' unsuccessful unarmed struggle against annihilation. He thought it was important to share the report with readers of

Hillel's newsletter *Clearing House,* whose readership extended far beyond the world of Hillel. Soon I was asked to lecture on the teaching of the Holocaust at a Boston conference of Hebrew school teachers.

The second paper, entitled "Silence in the American Textbooks," requires some explanation. It was the first of four publications, followed by the more significant and wider ranging convention article, which appeared in *Societas* (Summer 1972). Among other subjects, it discussed Arendt between 1944 and 1950, plus the emergence of the term "Holocaust." The paper ended with one quite important conclusion that YIVO's social scientist Nathan Reich commented on in his introduction to the *Societas* issue and that was also noted by Herbert S. Levine in his comments on the session: "For the present, it is fair enough to say that there is no Holocaust phenomenon in the historical writings of Clio's disciples in the United States, except among practitioners of Jewish history and Jewish intellectuals." The other two publications consisted of an anthology, *Hunter and Hunted,* which Viking Press originally published in 1973, and a case study entitled "Warsaw Plus Thirty: Some Perceptions in the Sources and Written History of the Ghetto Uprising" that appeared in the *YIVO Annual of Jewish Social Science* for 1974.

Like the paper I delivered at the convention, "Silence in the American Textbooks" had a Euro-American focus. In the context of important historiographical shifts during the 1960s in Germany, Israel, and the United States, it called on American-trained historians to place the Holocaust into the mainstream of Euro-American history by fashioning a new paradigm in presenting past gentile-Jewish relations. "Silence" was published in 1970 in volume three of *Yad Vashem Studies*—not that I was eager to have it first appear in Israel.

I had been unsuccessful in having it appear in a general American elite journal. Hennig Cohen, editor of *American Quarterly,* told me in a letter dated May 1968 that the editorial board felt I had failed "to focus in a direction that is suitable for our clientele," and that this was "not a fault of the manuscript itself." It was not his letter so much as the enclosed excerpt from one of his reader's reports that had stopped me cold: "The first textbook actually named and discussed at length is not on European history at all: it is Morison and Commager. And after a page or so we discover that the whole fault was in identifying Ann Frank as 'a little German girl.' [A year later, when Bill Leuchtenburg had joined the famous Morison and Commager team, Anne turned into a "little Jewish girl."] The case is further weakened by extensive summaries showing how cogently some textbooks do deal with Jews; and also by some unfortunate remarks on the influence of Christian culture . . . on historians."

A few months later, while on sabbatical leave from Cornell and teaching in the Department of History at Tel Aviv University, I showed the article to Livia Rothkirchen, the editor of *Yad Vashem Studies*. She accepted and promptly published it, first in the Hebrew edition and then in the English version, where quite a few scholars read it with appreciation.

One of these was David Patterson, the founding principal of the Oxford Centre for Hebrew and Jewish Studies. He and I became friends when David spent a couple of years at Cornell. We often discussed the Holocaust, and soon he suggested the possibility of compiling a Holocaust reader and publishing it in his B'nai B'rith Heritage Series, which Viking did in 1973. Another scholar was Reich, who was instrumental in arranging for the first panel discussion of the Holocaust at an annual meeting of the AHA.

Much has changed since then. In colleges and universities with an organized Jewish academic presence, the study of the Holocaust is important enough to be contentious; for some years now we have been reading about the "Shoah business." There are now priorities involving fund-raising, allocation of resources, and a balanced curriculum. Professional judgments vary over the relative significance of the Shoah in Israel and in the European and American Diaspora, about the relative importance of a mid-twentieth-century catastrophe compared to other periods, especially those far removed from our present world.

Although the beginnings of that change were already manifest in 1971, at the time I never considered my work as part of it—although, of course, it was. In small-town Ithaca—and, for that matter, among fellow historians at the Tel Aviv University, in 1968–69 and again in 1971–72—that erroneous perception was relatively easy to maintain. The reactions in Tel Aviv's history department surprised me. It turned out that those who had themselves lived through the catastrophe considered the subject part of their personal history; for they and their colleagues also thought of themselves as "secular" historians. To them I was the American historian, a published, tenured Cornell professor who had been asked to join the department in order to help establish an American history section. The Shoah belonged to the university's well-known Jewish historians, members of a different department specializing in Jewish subjects, who were housed in a different building.

Even as the Holocaust was institutionalized in the United States, with Holocaust studies as a professional discipline, my later "Holocaust" publications retained their original focus, namely, that of an American historian responding to personal and professional experiences, calling on colleagues to be sensitive to another historical phenomenon in European and American history. To be sure, given that orientation, on occasion I strayed into the substantive history of the Shoah and its immediate aftermath, but I did so reluctantly. I did not have the ability, nor the language skills or religious training, to work exclusively among so many different kinds of Holocaust sources, including rabbinic *Responsa* of the kind that are to be found in Ephraim Oshry's *Mimaamakim.* Besides, I did not have the emotional strength or mental discipline to work fulltime on the Holocaust and also help rear my own optimistic and action-oriented Jewish family.

For a while, in the 1960s and early 1970s, I felt alone in publicly maintaining this "Holocaust" focus in Ithaca and among my U.S. colleagues in the history profession. I also sensed I could not really be alone: surely somewhere in the profession there had to be American colleagues who could comprehend the Holocaust as a subject fit for serious investigation, as something more than a Jewish subject promulgated and nurtured, as critics then claimed, by self-appointed, parochially minded "victim historians" demanding unwarranted public recognition for themselves and their people's suffering.

Indeed, as I learned in 1971, I was not alone.[5] But it was not until 2000 that I read with a deep sense of pride that the master historian I so admired had also been there. George Mosse, ever Clio's devoted servant, wrote the following lines in his memoir about himself and the Holocaust: "All my studies of racism and volkish thought, and also those dealing with outsiderdom and stereotypes, though sometimes not directly related to the Holocaust, have tried to find an answer to how it could have happened; finding an explanation has been vital not only for the understanding of modern history, but also for my own peace of mind. This is a question my generation had to face, and eventually I felt that I had come closer to an understanding of the Holocaust as a historical phenomenon."[6]

It is this darker side of our history that prompted me to entitle my American immigration narrative *Nightmare's Fairy Tale*. Surely it is linked to Jewish cinders, now commingled with the black salt of the Atlantic Ocean and the red dust of the American prairie.

Acknowledgments

Notes

Index

Aboard a whale-watch vessel in Boston harbor, in celebration of the author's seventy-fifth birthday in 2003. The photo shows Ann Sandford, my children, Arona, Malkie, Ezra, Joshua, and some of theirs, including Avital, Raphael, Moshe, Aviad, and Jaime.

Acknowledgments

I owe many debts to various individuals, but some are admittedly special. Elie Wiesel, David Patterson, Bob Marshall, Steve Katz, and Harvey Fireside offered helpful suggestions when I needed them. Former students Mark Blaifeder, George Hiltzik, Lynn Paltrow, and Bill Schechter made insightful comments about earlier drafts of the manuscript. Robert Mandel and his editorial staff at the University of Wisconsin Press, and Donald Dietrich, at Boston College, read the manuscript carefully; I benefited from their detailed critical judgments. John McClymer, my friend and lunch partner at Assumption College in Worcester, Mass., suggested judicious pruning of the text. My nephews, Cliff and Jerry, helpfully pointed out passages that confused them. My children—Arona, Joshua, Ezra, and Malka—weeded out errors and pointed out omissions. I am grateful to all for their enthusiasm.

When I was forced to rely on memory alone, my brother, Manfred—who is such an integral part of this story—offered second opinions; he remains as always a constant source of joy and support. Fellow historian Ann Sandford, my best friend and longtime partner, gave me a special gift: her sense of place, in our home and garden, a retreat for the writing of this story.

An act of homage "shows respect or attests to the worth or influence of another." I was honored by the friendship and counsel of the late Paul Gates. Long ago this grand master among American historians reacted uniquely—and unforgettably—to my 1971 article about our colleagues and their response to the Holocaust. As we crossed Cornell's arts quad, he said: "Knowing what you know, why don't you scream all the time." Were it not for the understanding of teachers and friends, I would not have written this improbable story. Next to my family and loved ones, I owe them everything. They made me feel privileged in the neighborhoods where I lived, at the schools where I studied, and at the institutions where I taught.

Notes

Chapter 1

1. Gerd Korman, ed., *Hunter and Hunted: Human History of the Holocaust* (New York: Viking, 1973), 305-7.

2. Ruth Gosling, Talaton, to Kormans, Brooklyn, Dec. 18, 1945, in the Korman Papers, Cornell University Archives. All correspondence cited are in this collection or in the possession of the author. I have spelled the family name Korman with just one "n."

Chapter 2

1. The events leading up to and following the deportation are described in *"St. Louis:* An Eventful Experience of a Passenger," a brief manuscript written after 1946 by Max Korman. Families were not invariably rounded up together. See also Miriam Gillis-Carlebach, *Jedes Kind ist mein Einziges* (Hamburg: Dölling und Galitz, 1992), 209-10.

2. Between 1939 and 1944 I filled composition notebooks with three different versions ("Das Los Der 'Juden,'" "America My Hope," and "Make Palestine a Haven for Jewish Refugees") of the deportation and other experiences during those years. One of them records "committee" members coming through the train in Hamburg with boxes of food. It is possible that the scene with the oranges also occurred before dawn, when we stopped briefly in Berlin. In prison we had been given a bowl of pea soup for lunch, but it was not kosher, so many did not eat it. See also Gillis-Carlebach, *Jedes Kind ist mein Einziges,* 209-10.

3. See Sybil Milton, "The Expulsion of Polish Jews from Germany, October 1938 to July 1939," *Leo Baeck Year Book* 29 (1984): 169-74, 182, 186, 187; "Menschen zwischen Grenzen: Die Polen ausweisung 1938," *Menora Jahrbuch für deutsch-jüdische Geschichte, 1990,* 184-85, 192-93, 197; Karol Jonca, "The Expulsion of Polish Jews from the Third Reich in 1938," *Polin* 8 (1994): 255-81. On September 9, 1933, Pappi was charged with insulting the German state or the Wehrmacht—he was later found not guilty—for spitting into the gutter of a

street in the town of Itzehoe, where some distance away stood a military motorcycle bearing a Nazi flag. Personal communication from Landesarchiv Schleswig-Holstein to Gerd Korman, March 3, 1994.

4. See Milton, "The Expulsion of Polish Jews from Germany," 190–95. See also related documents from Polish authorities in Jonca, "The Expulsion of Polish Jews from the Third Reich," 255–81. Lastly, see Trude Maurer's "Abschiebung und Attentat: Die Ausweisung der polnischen Juden und der Vorwand für die 'Kristallnacht,'" in Walter H. Pehle, ed., *Der Judenpogrom 1938* (Frankfurt am Main: Fischer, 1988); there is an English translation by Struan Roberts at http://www.ITZ, uni-hamburg.de/rz3a035.

5. Some of these details are from a fragmentary memoir entitled "Narol," which was written around 1994 by one of my cousins, Norbert Korman, the son of my Uncle Wolf and his wife Deborah Fogel.

6. For a partial list of names of those deported from Hamburg-Altona to Zbaszyn, see Jürgen Sielemann and Paul Flamme, eds., *Hamburger jüdische Opfer des Nationalsozialismus: Gedenkbuch*, vol. 15 (Hamburg: Staatsachiv, 1995), xvii–xviii. Many details concerning our belongings on the Behnstrasse and the deportation and its aftermath may be found in the following sources: Akte der Devisenstelle Hamburg (314–15 Oberfinanzpräident, FVg7177) and Akte des Rechtanwalt Dr. Siegfried Urias (621–1, 19), Staatsarchiv, Hamburg. I am grateful to Jürgen Sielemann for forwarding copies of these documents.

7. For an official account of his murder, accompanied by clippings from the Nazi press, see the following police report of the killing: No.5/673, Bestand: Landgericht, Elberfeld, Staaatsarchiv, Düsseldorf. See also: David Magnus Mintert, *"Sturmtrupp der Deutschen Republik": Das Reichsbanner Schwarz-Rot-Gold im Wuppertal* (Wuppertal: Forschungsgruppe Wuppertaler Wiederstand, 2002), 116; Hans-Helmuth Knütter, "Die Linksparteien," and Arnold Paucker, "Der jüdische Abwehrkampf," in Werner E. Mosse, ed., *Entscheidungsjahr, 1932* (Tübingen: J. C. B. Mohr, 1966), 323–345, 452–453; and Gerhart Werner, "Über den Wiederstand in Wuppertal," in Gerhart Werner, ed., *Aufmachen! Gestapo!* (Wuppertal: Presse und Werbeamt, 1974), 10–14.

8. Milton, "The Expulsion of Polish Jews from Germany," 190–95.

Chapter 3

1. See Milton, "The Expulsion of Polish Jews from Germany," 195–98. Jürgen Sielemann and Paul Flamme claim that people like Pappi who returned to Hamburg were expected to emigrate within the allotted time. Many failed, and shortly after the start of the war they were rounded up and sent to the local concentration camp in Fuhlsbüttel. See Sielemann and Flamme, eds., *Hamburger jüdische Opfer des Nationalsozialismus*, xvii–xxviii.

2. Personal correspondence from Selma W. Basker, Immigration Chairman, National Council of Jewish Women, Miami Section, to O. Korman, February 4 & 8, 1939.

3. Max Korman, Hamburg, to Selma W. Basker, Miami, April 23, 1939; Douglas Jenkins Jr., American Vice-Consul in Warsaw, to Osias Korman, Hamburg, May 2, 1939; and William H. Cordell, American Vice-Consul in Warsaw,

to Rosa Korman, Zbaszyn, April 4, 1939. In a letter from D. Guzik of the Polish branch of the JDC, DGP.No.2319, Warsaw, to O. Korman, Hamburg, April 18, 1939, he informs him of his frustrated efforts in dealing with the American consul and asks him to address his correspondence not to specific individuals but "just to the Organization."

4. Max Korman, "*St. Louis:* An Eventful Experience of a Passenger."

5. Max Korman, Amsterdam, to Rosa Korman, Zbaszyn, quoted in G. Korman, ed., *Hunter and Hunted,* 48; Baruch Weissman, Havana, to Max Korman, Amsterdam, June 29, 1939; and Max Korman (aboard the *St. Louis*) to Rosa Korman, Zbaszyn, May 18, 1939.

6. G. Korman, ed., *Hunter and Hunted,* 49–52.

7. See Louise London, *Whitehall and the Jew, 1933–1948: British Immigration Policy, Jewish Refugees and the Holocaust* (New York: Cambridge University Press, 2000), 137–38; G. Korman, ed., *Hunter and Hunted,* 55. See also A. J. Sherman, *Island Refuge: Britain and Refugees from the Third Reich, 1933–1939* (Ilford, UK: Frank Cass, 1994), 252–53.

8. There had been a number of earlier transports from Zbaszyn to London. See Barry Turner, . . . *And the Policeman Smiled: 10,000 Children Escape from Nazi Europe* (London: Bloomsbury, 1990), 90–91.

9. J. Goldberg, Esq., London, to Osias Korman, Hamburg, May 5, 1939.

Chapter 4

1. Osias Korman, Amsterdam, to Selma Basker, Miami, September 19, 1939; Selma Basker, Miami, to Rosa Korman, Elberfeld, November 16, 1939; Osias Engelberg, Miami, to Osias Korman, Westerbork, January 1, 1940.

2. Osias Korman, Amsterdam, to Comite voor bijzondere Joodische Belangen, July 17, 1939.

3. Osias Korman, Amsterdam, to the American consulate, Hamburg, August 2, 1939; Osias Korman, Amsterdam, to the American consulate, Amsterdam, August 3, 1939.

4. Osias Korman, Amsterdam, to the Polish Refugee Committee, London, August 13, 1939.

5. Copy of Rosa, Gerd, and Manfred Korman files obtained from the U.S. Citizenship and Immigration Services, Department of Homeland Security; Rosa Korman, Hamburg, to Max Korman, Amsterdam, August 23, 1939. The consulate did not issue the visa until early 1940, after his demands for increased deposits in Mutti's name and a supplementary affidavit had been filed for her and her children.

6. Gerd Korman, "Das Los Der 'Juden,'" "America My Hope," and "Make Palestine a Haven for Jewish Refugees." Shortly after we left, the hostel was destroyed in a German air raid; Willie Nayman to Gerd Korman, December 14, 1994.

7. Oral communication from Mrs. Kamiel, August 1967; Gerd Korman, Talaton, to Osias Korman, Amsterdam, n.d. (before September 27, 1939).

8. Gerd Korman, Talaton, to Pappi, Amsterdam, n.d. (before September 27, 1939). Children from other transports that had sailed from Gdinya on the

Warszawa before us reported traumatic delousing experiences before embarking. See the recollection by the then ten-year-old Harry Katz in Turner, *And the Policeman Smiled,* 91.

9. Gerd Korman, Talaton, to "Liebe Mutti," Elberfeld, October 16, 1939. The correspondence from England to Germany went via Pappi in then still neutral Holland.

10. Unfortunately, I have not been able to trace the paper trail leading to this family.

Chapter 5

1. For background information and relevant details about the war, I have relied upon the following: John Keegan, *The Second World War* (New York: Penguin, 1990); Ernest R. May, *Strange Victory: Hitler's Conquest of France* (New York: Hill and Wang, 2000); and Gerhard L. Weinberg, *A World at Arms: A Global History of World War II* (New York: Cambridge University Press, 1994).

2. U.S. neutrality legislation resulted in the reassignment of shipping routes for American carriers to Italy from England, Ireland, France, and Germany.

3. See Turner, *And the Policeman Smiled,* 143–55. The story of the Christian children was featured on an episode of CBS's *60 Minutes* in 1999 and again in 2002.

4. Osias Korman, Amsterdam, to Selma Basker, Miami, September 19, 1939; Selma Basker, Miami, to Rosa Korman, Elberfeld, November 16, 1939; Osias Engelberg, Miami, to Osias Korman, Westerbork, January 1, 1940.

5. Max Korman, Westerbork, to Rosa Korman, Elberfeld, April 11, 1940. Mutti's postcard to Talaton was mailed from New York on April 30, 1940. See also Rosa Korman file, Department of Homeland Security, and May, *Strange Victory,* 414–16.

6. Gerd Korman, Talaton, to "Liebe Mammi," Brooklyn, April 26, 1940.

7. Ibid. Charoset, a mixture of nuts, apples, and wine meant to represent clay for making bricks.

Chapter 6

1. Undated letter addressed to "Dear Mummie."

2. Gerd Korman, London, to "Liebe Mummi," New York, May 7, 1940. We each obtained our Certificate of Identity from the Home Office on July 15 and the visa from the American consulate on July 26, 1940.

3. See David Dyrett, *The Defeat of the German U-Boats: The Battle of the Atlantic* (Columbia: University of South Carolina Press, 1994), 8.

4. Gerd Korman, Brooklyn, to Lieber Pappi, Amsterdam, September 11, 1940.

5. Mutti received two telegrams, one from the Marine Department at the port and another from me.

6. Oral communication with Bee Engelberg, Miami, Thanksgiving 1989.

7. Gerd Korman, Brooklyn, to Lieber Pappi, Amsterdam, November 9, 1940.

Chapter 7

1. Erich Cohn, Chairman, Executive Committee of the Jewish Congregation in Camp Westerbork, to Osias Korman, "hier," Amsterdam, March 10, 1941.

2. "Vater," Westerbork, to "Lieber Gerd!," Brooklyn, June 24, 1941. There were other letters from friends in New York. One came from Helene Schaffer, the wife of Sigmund, who had tried to bring Pappi to England after the *St. Louis* docked in Antwerp.

3. We were still at it during our last semester in spring 1947. According to my U.S. tax withholding statement for 1947, I earned $66 delivering papers, on which I paid $0.60 income tax. My total income for that year was $1,537.60, most of which was earned in a full-time job at the StarLight Company. I kept about $260 for pocket money, leaving some $1,277 for family income.

4. Between 1944 and 1948 I was often mentioned in the sports columns of *Aufbau,* the German-language weekly published by the New World Club.

5. In June 1944 the league adopted special rules barring antisemitic outbursts on the playing field. See *Aufbau,* June 2 and 22, 1944.

6. For a general background of World War II in the United States I have turned to John Morton Blum, *V Was for Victory: Politics and American Culture during World War II* (New York: Harcourt Brace Jovanovich, 1976). Cilli's despondent husband, Samuel, died during the war. A daughter and son had immigrated to Palestine, the son (also named Manfred) becoming a soldier in the Palestine Brigade and ultimately a prisoner of war.

7. On March 7, 1942, I wrote Mutti in Miami Beach. Her employers from Great Neck had taken her with them to look after the children during their extended vacation. I asked her to write the Kormans to make certain we could come. On March 22 Manfred wrote, asking if Mutti had told the Kormans we were coming. Later, in an undated note, I told her we had spent the Passover seders at the Kormans.

8. John Petrover, Brooklyn, to O. Engelberg, Miami Beach, December 15, 1940. Actually, his own statement showed that he had agreed to take us for $40, upped it in October to $60, and reduced it in November to $55. According to his records, starting in October my mother had paid part of her debts in small amounts ranging from $15 on October 3 to $5 on November 21 and $30 on December 2. By then she had paid a total of $100.

9. John Petrover, Brooklyn, to O. Engelberg, Brooklyn, January 21 and February 2, 1941, with notes from the uncle and granddaughter.

Chapter 8

1. Max Korman's recollections from 1962 are quoted in G. Korman, ed., *Hunter and Hunted,* 274; see also, in same source, Walter Lenz's recollections, 267–69. I have also read photocopies of some of the papers of Rabbi Capt. Samuel Cass. Between April 11 and June 4, 1945, he visited liberated Westerbork frequently and wrote to my mother in Brooklyn. The papers are housed in the Canadian National Archives, Ottawa, under MG 30, D225; volumes 6–9 contain a

number of files with diary entries, official reports, and some notes and letters involving Westerbork and my father.

2. Augusta Myerson, National Refugee Service, New York City, to Rosa Korman, September 23, 1940; E. E. Salisbury, Chief Certification Branch, for Henry M. Hart, Jr., Special Assistant to the Attorney General in Charge Pro Tem, Immigration and Naturalization Service, U.S. Department of Justice, to H. Henry Steinberg [attorney at law], Brooklyn, December 21, 1940.

3. A. Einstein to Frau Rosa Korman, January 14, 1941, and November 29, 1945. He also responded on his sixty-fifth birthday with a printed card, thanking Mutti for her "kind condolences upon my 65th birthday."

4. See Leonard Dinnerstein, *America and the Survivors of the Holocaust* (New York: Columbia University Press, 1982), esp. 117–271.

5. E. H. Wipperman, Asst. Sec., Manufacturers Trust Co., Brooklyn, to American Consul in Amsterdam, October 1 and November 26, 1945; Affidavit of Support by Rosa Korman, December 3, 1945.

6. Notarized financial statements of M. Kopit, December 4, 1945; Morris Kopit's U.S. income tax return for 1944.

7. Joseph Savoretti to Rosa L. Korman, c/o Mrs. Esther B. Kaunitz, Director, National Council of Jewish Women, New York, January 29, 1946.

8. See A. de Vries, Director, Jewish Coordinating Committee, June 20, 1945, where he states that "Osyas" Korman worked in his office "as head of the administration from November 1, 1945, to June 1, 1946."

9. Dorothy L. Speiser, Assistant Treasurer, Joint Distribution Committee, to Rosa Korman, November 13, 1964. See also the file of Osias Korman in the "St. Louis Project" of the U.S. Holocaust Museum. I have a photocopy of that file.

10. By April 10, 1946, he had his visa and was trying to book passage.

11. Forty dollars may be a bit high. In 1949 she reported an annual income of $2,149 based on her having worked for twenty different families.

Chapter 9

1. See "Children Transport" in local contemporary newspaper clippings for the names and U.S. destinations of these passengers.

2. The above passages are based on the following: memoranda and notices from Westerbork officials; letters written by Pappi; letters and diary entries written by Etty Hillesum; conversations with Pappi and his friends Cohn, Walter Lenz, and Liesel Levy; and a doctor's report written one year after he had died of a heart attack in 1962. For studies of Westerbork, see Jacob Boas, *Boulevard des Misères: The Story of Transit Camp Westerbork* (Hamden, Conn.: Archon Press, 1985); Jacob Presser, *The Destruction of Dutch Jews* (New York: Dutton, 1969). See also the comments of Liesel Levy in Etty Hillesum, *Etty: De nagelaten geschriften van Etty Hillesum, 1941–1943* (Amsterdam: Uitgeverij Balans, 1986), 779. I have used Harold Fisch's translation of the passages Pappi quoted from Ecclesiastes 9:2–4.

3. Pappi's papers include receipts from garages and hotels where he had stopped in 1947 when he worked for the Wiggletoe Shoe Company of Newark,

N.J. Within one year he drove about eighty-five hundred miles. His tax return for 1947 lists $25.35 as earned income from the electrochemical firm and $2,138.92 from Wiggletoe. By the end of 1947 he was still losing money as a shoe salesman, but this did not prevent him and Mutti—who, with her forty dollars a week, was still our main provider—from sending small charitable contributions to the UJA Emergency Campaign for Refugee Children. In mid-September 1946 Pappi purchased our first family insurance in the United States; membership in the Associated Hospital Service of New York cost $6.60 per quarter.

4. Turner, *And the Policeman Smiled*, 243.

5. Ibid., 244–46; oral communication with Yossel's sister Sarah in Kibbutz Hefziba, Israel, August 1993. At the end of 1945 (or possibly 1946) Ruth Gosling wrote us that "Paula lives in Torquay, Isa works in Honiton . . . ; she is engaged to a bus driver!"

6. Oral communications with Yossel, August 1967.

7. On December 18, 1945, Ruth Gosling wrote us that "Joe is going to London on Dec. 29th to see a rabbi who was in the camp where Joe's mother as [sic] sister is in Germany it will be very nice for Joe to here [sic] all about his mother."

Chapter 10

1. The Yiddish daily *Forward* and the AJC's *Committee Reporter* printed a photograph of the three of us with Raymond Massey and former governor Lehman. The caption identified Manfred as a "refugee boy," Mutti as "Mrs. Osias Korman, a refugee wife," and Gerhardt as "Mrs. Korman's second son."

Chapter 11

1. Morton Wishengrad, "The Bitter Herb," typescript copy, April 2, 1947, pp. 7, 12. This copy, distributed by the American Jewish Committee, included former governor Lehman's brief address. In it he appealed to America to "admit our fair share of . . . victims of Nazism to our shores," but he was explicitly speaking of 650,000 "Roman Catholics, Greek Catholics and Protestants" and of some 200,000 Jews (13).

Epilogue

1. An example of slave-trade documents can be found in Merrill Jensen, ed., *American Colonial Documents to 1776* (London: Eyre & Spottiswoode, 1955), 495–504. G. Korman, ed., *Hunter and Hunted*, 264, reprints the Nazi document. See also Eugen Kogon, *Der SS-Staat: Das System der deutschen Konzentrationslager* (Munich: Verlag Karl Alber, 1946), 296–97.

2. George Kennan, *Memoirs, 1935–1950* (New York: Bantam, 1968), 114; see also 112–17, 124–28, 138–39.

3. George L. Mosse, *Confronting History: A Memoir* (Madison: University of Wisconsin Press, 2000), 219.

4. Gerd Korman, "The Holocaust in American Historical Writing," *Societas* 2 (Summer 1972): 268, note 37.

5. See especially Henry L. Feingold, *The Politics of Rescue: The Roosevelt Administration and the Holocaust* (New Brunswick, N.J.: Rutgers University Press, 1970).

6. Mosse, *Confronting History.* 219.

Index

MALKA KORMAN STEYN
1966–2005

Shalom oh Sun
Shalom oh Light

Dusk comes
And then the Night

SHOAH STUDIES

. . . And Heaven Shed No Tears
Henry Armin Herzog

Nightmare's Fairy Tale
Gerd Korman